WALKERS, WRITERS & WATERING HOLES

WALKERS, Writers & WATERING HOLES

A GENTLE WANDER DOWN WHARFEDALE

by
Barrie Pepper and Jack Thompson

Wharncliffe Publishing

First Published in 2000 by
Wharncliffe Publishing
an imprint of
Pen and Sword Books Limited,
47 Church Street, Barnsley,
South Yorkshire. S70 2AS

For up-to-date information on other titles produced under the
Wharncliffe imprint, please telephone or write to:

> **Wharncliffe Publishing**
> **FREEPOST**
> **47 Church Street**
> **Barnsley**
> **South Yorkshire S70 2BR**
> **Telephone (24 hours): 01226 - 734555**

ISBN: 1-871647-86-X

A CIP catalogue record of this book is available from the
British Library

Cover illustration: Hubberholme

Printed in Great Britain by
Redwood Books, Trowbridge, Wiltshire

CONTENTS

A village inn is not simply a place where one goes for food and drink and lodging, as one goes to a hotel in the city. It is an integral part of the village, and the dale in which it stands. It has a character of its own, which it has acquired through years – and sometimes through centuries – of its existence. The old innkeepers appreciated and treasured this tradition; they became part and parcel of the inn itself. They were proud of their heritage and jealous of their reputations. The inn to them was a sacred trust.

Alfred J Brown, Broad Acres

$\mathcal{F}$ORWARD

I grew up in Burley in Wharfedale. Many an idyllic summer's day I can recall eating crisps and drinking lemonade with my brothers in the car whilst my parents had a quick drink at one of the local pubs featured in this guide. As a teenager, long walks in the upper reaches of the dale gave me an enduring feel of rural Yorkshire and a sense of how important the local village pub is to both visitors and residents alike.

Today, I represent in Parliament the southern sections of the dale from Tadcaster to Cawood. It is my ambition to visit every pub in my constituency and *Walkers, Writers & Watering Holes* will certainly help in my task.

Whether you are primarily a rambler, a connoisseur of beer or a tourist you could have picked no better guide to the pubs of Wharfedale than Barrie Pepper and Jack Thompson's book. Sample some of the fare on offer not least because the inns you will visit will give a real feel of the Yorkshire identity. One day I will choose one of them to stay in and after a hearty meal and a good night's sleep, will travel through Wharfedale on a summer's morning to the first day of the Headingley test match. Life could not get much better.

John Grogan,
Member of Parliament for Selby

*I*NTRODUCTION

The River Wharfe rises in the Pennines on Cam Fell in Langstrothdale and runs 69 miles from there to Wharfe's Mouth near Cawood where it enters the River Ouse. Wharfe is an old British word for winding although another claim is that is from the Saxon word guerf meaning swift. And along this winding, swift, wandering river there is the most magnificent selection of inns and public houses in some of the most delightful hamlets, villages and small towns of Yorkshire. And they are near to many places of interest which makes a journey through all or any part of the dale a satisfying, enlightening and fascinating experience.

At our last count we checked off 150 pubs in Wharfedale taking in some minor diversions from the main dale and not including private hotels and guest houses which may be licensed. And in the firm belief that the best beers are cask conditioned ones - real ales - we have merely noted any pubs that do not supply them. They are few and far between and we only found two. Many of Wharfedales pubs are historic, a few are modern, but most are of interest and have something to offer and often tales to tell.

The River Wharfe is paralleled by good roads (Addingham to Towton is on A class roads) but it is not too well served by public transport although this situation is improving. In the lower part of the dale there are bus links between the major villages and towns but few continuous services and there are only regular ones in the upper section of the valley during the summer. Information about bus services is given where appropriate but changes are frequent so it is always advisable to check and a list of the companies operating in the area is supplied with their telephone numbers. A short section of the Leeds to Ilkley railway line follows the valley and the main line from Leeds to York passes through Church Fenton and Ulleskelf. The Dales Way long distance footpath follows the river from near its source at Cam Houses where it has a junction with the Pennine Way as far as Ilkley, and the Ebor Way can be walked along the river from Harewood to Tadcaster.

This well illustrated guide gives you a good idea of the facilities available at most of the pubs in Wharfedale and sometimes a little of their history. Some are linked together to make up interesting pub crawls and pleasant walks. Historic and artistic connections are found and the book also selects appropriate tourist attractions and gives the reader some useful travel information. And, if after all this, you fancy a cup of tea then there is even a list of tea shops.

Barrie Pepper and Jack Thompson

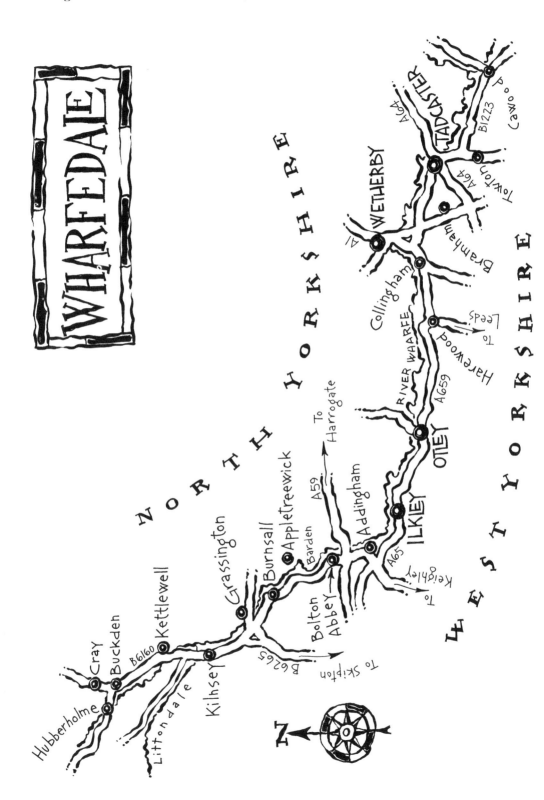

Opening Time – The Source Of The Wharfe & The Dale's First Watering Holes

Wharfe threads it all with her glamour, ever-changing melody. She can make music out of the harshest odds, or sing quiet songs of faëry.

Halliwell Sutcliffe, The Striding Dales.

Finding the source of rivers is an enticing and everlasting affair. No one can really tell where they start; only where they finish. Several streams join a main one and who is to say which one of these children is the eldest that spawns the real source? However most writers, historians and lovers of the dales agree that the River Wharfe starts out from Cam Fell close to Gayle Moor where the red rose Ribble also finds its beginnings.

In its first meanderings as Oughtershaw Beck it links with Green Field Beck at Beckermonds where the writer A J Brown says 'Wharfe is born'. From here it takes its leisurely course through Langstrothdale Chase passing Deepdale which in 1613 had two inns to service its populace and Yockenthwaite where there is a well preserved Bronze Age stone circle. Dr Whittaker in his History of Craven described the Wharfe as: 'issuing from a meagre spring on the margin of a bog, after the progress of a few miles, becomes a noble and animated river, exasperated by rocks or precipitated into cataracts...'

While Wharfedale these days flows through North Yorkshire into the metropolitan districts of Bradford and Leeds and back into North Yorkshire again prior to 1974 it was entirely in the West Riding of Yorkshire.

The first inn of modern day Wharfedale is **The George** at Hubberholme - often pronounced Ubram. It nestles at the foot of the hills by the bridge. This

The George at Hubberholme – JB Priestley's favourite pub.

'J B Priestley, O.M., 1894 - 1984. Author and Dramatist, whose ashes are buried nearby. He loved the Dales and found Hubberholme one of the smallest and pleasantest places in the world.'

MEMORIAL TABLET IN HUBBERHOLME CHURCH

John Boynton Priestley was born in Bradford, the son of a schoolmaster, and after serving in the infantry during World War I in which he was wounded three times he graduated at Trinity Hall, Cambridge. He first worked as journalist in London and moved on to achieve an international reputation as an essayist, critic, author and dramatist. His attitudes towards society showed through in his work displaying his practical socialism, opposition to materialism and love of his fellow man. He wrote the popular novels *The Good Companions* and *Angel Pavement* and then he moved into drama with such plays as *Dangerous Corner, I Have Been Here Before* and *An Inspector Calls*. The plays were experimental in their treatment of time but he also wrote the Yorkshire comedy *When We Are Married*. His non fiction work included *An English Journey, Literature and Western Man, Man and Time* and *The Edwardians*. He married the archaeologist and writer Jacquetta Hawkes. After declining a knighthood and a peerage, he accepted the Order of Merit from Queen Elizabeth II in 1977. He was made a freeman of his native city in 1980 which in the view of many folk was far later than he deserved. He died in 1984 after a short illness and a good life. Hubberholme was his favourite spot in the Dales. He wrote:

'Here there is space and beauty. The elements seem to be balanced; the earth seems to touch the sky.'

eighteenth-century white-washed pub was a farmhouse in its early days and later the vicarage for the neighbouring St Michael's church. Pub, church and bridge form Yorkshire's smallest conservation area.A former landlady, Grace Pawson, is said to have kept a large stick to control her drunken and unruly customers. The pub still retains its stone-flagged floors, open fires, and mullion windows. Food is served at all sessions and the blackboard menu has English, Thai and vegetarian dishes, home-made pies and soups. The beers available include Black Sheep Special and Tetley Mild and Bitter. The pub closes in the afternoons except at weekends and on 'sunny' Mondays. There are seven letting bedrooms with well priced winter breaks and a small camp site. (Telephone 01756 760223).

Take time to visit the beautiful Norman church which has the only remaining rood loft in the former West Riding which dates from 1558, a rare polygonal font and stalls built and carved by Robert 'Mousey' Thompson of Kilburn. And view the memorial to the author J B Priestley who regarded the village as one of the smallest and pleasantest places in the world and claimed the George as one of his favourite pubs. He wrote: 'In summer, long after the snows had melted, there is rarely much water in the river, so that it glitters and winks; and a man who has been walking for an hour or two can loiter on that bridge for quite a time, waiting for the pub to open and staring at the river.'

The White Lion at Cray – Wharfedale's highest pub.

High above Hubberholme is **The White Lion** at Cray a seventeenth century inn and, at 1,200 feet above sea level, the highest in Wharfedale. At one time it was used by packhorse traders and drovers taking their cattle to markets in the midlands and London. Walkers are welcome here but you are expected to leave muddy boots outside. There is an open fire and stone flagged floors and the walls are covered with old farming implements. The interesting old pub game of Ring the Bull or Bull 'ook is played here. The beers are Moorhouse Black Cat, Premier and Pendle Witch, Rooster Yankee, Black Sheep Best Bitter and occasional guests. Food is served in the bar and the non-smoking dining room both at lunchtimes and evenings with an 'early bird' menu up to 6.15 pm. There are some sophisticated dishes on the menu and lots of good plain food including casseroles and large Yorkshire puddings with various fillings. Outdoor drinking and eating is popular in the pretty garden or even alongside the tumbling stream across the road. The pub is open all day. There are eight rooms for bed and breakfast with some generous offers in the off season. (Telephone: 01756 760262). According to Helliwell Sutcliffe in *The Striding Dales*: 'To sleep in this inn is to awake next morning to a sense of spacious ease. The air blows sweet from the massive bulk of Buckden Pike; and everywhere there is the roar and bubble of descending waters.'

Below in the valley bottom is **The Buck** at Buckden, a splendid stone-faced country inn which faces the sloping village green of this increasingly popular village. It was here at Christmas in 1945 that the future cabinet minister Denis Healey and his wife Edna (now Lord and Lady Healey) spent their honeymoon in the loft of an adjoining barn, there being no room at the inn. Things are a little different these days and The Buck is noted for its comfortable accommodation

The Buck in Buckden – where the Healey's honeymooned in a loft.

with 14 en-suite bedrooms including one with a four-poster bed and a suite (01756 760227). There is a bar and restaurant, open fires and cosy seating. On sale are a full range of Theakston's ales - Best Bitter, Black Bull, XB and Old Peculier - and occasional guest beers and the bar is open all day. There is bar food at all sessions except Sunday evenings and a full restaurant service from 6 pm to 9 pm. Morning coffee and afternoon tea is available. Priestley said Buckden was a notable goal for Bradfordians: 'who have emptied the barrels at the inn there many a time.' The pub closes for two weeks in early January.

Two miles along the main road is **The Fox and Hounds** (01756 760269) in the pleasant limestone village of Starbotton, a welcoming inn dating from 1834 with low beams, flagged floors and open fires. The building itself goes back more than 400 years. There is an amusing sign showing a hunt in progress with the fox getting very much the better of the hounds. The pub serves above the average good value pub food (it is a regular entry in *Good Pub Food*) with its own freshly baked bread and a menu including several vegetarian and vegan choices. Handpumped beers include Taylor Landlord, Theakston Black Bull and Old Peculier and Black Sheep Best Bitter with guest beers during the summer months. There are also two letting bedrooms. In summer the pub closes during the afternoons and on Mondays except bank holiday lunchtimes. In winter it shuts down during January and the first half of February and it is best to check its availability by phoning. The pub is a useful starting point for walking sections of the Dales Way and the recommended ramble that follows. It has a sizeable car park but one needs to seek the approval of the licensee to use it whilst away from the pub.

$\mathcal{A}$ Pub Crawl Through Upper Wharfedale

$\mathcal{T}$hese four pubs combine to make a pleasant circular ramble through Upper Wharfedale which at most is seven miles long and not too arduous. The best starting point is at Starbotton. From the pub turn left on the main road towards Kettlewell - 300 yards along on your right is a footpath sign to Buckden. Go down a disused cart track and cross the River Wharfe by a footbridge then turn right and follow the river bank for 500 yards. The path then leaves the river and goes through meadows and alongside Firth Woods. In spring and summer there are many varieties of birds along this stretch and walkers have been rewarded by sightings of buzzards and more common birds such as curlews, mallards, shovellers and dippers. At Birks Wood the path rejoins the river and it is a flat easy walk to the bridge at Buckden. At this point you have a choice of routes, turning left and using the road or crossing the road and continuing to follow the footpath by the river. Both routes lead to Hubberholme.

After calling in at the church go along the road on the north side of the river and just before a road junction take the footpath and the fairly stiff climb up Cray Gill with views of the waterfalls on the left. You will soon arrive in Cray.

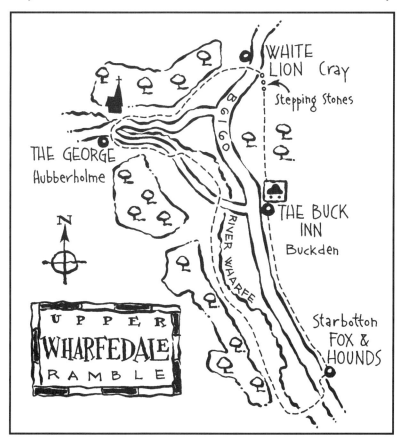

THE HUBBERHOLME RENT AUCTION OR LAND-LETTING

Behind the George is a sixteen acre field known as Poor Pasture, which is let off by auction on the first Monday in each New Year. Its origins are not known but the way it is conducted by an auction, the duration of which is determined by the burning of a candle, was a popular practice in the eighteenth century. The sale starts with a short service in the church and then continues in the inn with a ceremony sometimes called the Hubberholme Parliament with the 'Lords' - the vicar, who acts as the auctioneer, his churchwardens and the past tenant, and the 'Commons' - the bidders. The candle is lit at 8 pm and usually burns for around four hours during which time the landlord feeds the assembled company. At first the bidding is a bit of a joke but towards midnight only those farmers who want the field to graze their sheep take it seriously. The proceeds are given to the sick and poor of the parish.

From the White Lion cross the road and the stream by the stepping stones and follow the footpath signs for Buckden. There is a short sharp climb to join the ridge path which turns right along a well defined track which drops through Rakes Wood and ends up in Buckden car park. From the ridge the views over Upper Wharfedale are magnificent. If you have travelled by bus from the Skipton direction it is possible to end the ramble here and return south, or you can continue a further two miles along the main road back to Starbotton. The flexibility of this crawl is entirely with the walker. Read it as you wish, but enjoy it.

It is essentially a summer walk particularly if you use the bus services up the valley for out of season they are, to say the least, irregular. In addition to the pubs it takes in a delightful riverside walk, much of it on the Dales Way, lots of interesting wild life and some spectacular views. OS map 98 (Wensleydale and Upper Wharfedale) or Touring map 6 (Yorkshire Dales) are helpful. Information on bus services can be obtained from Keighley and District Transport on 01535 603284 or Pride of the Dales on 01756 753123. School bus services also take other passengers but do not run out of term times. It is best to plan the route carefully bearing in mind the opening hours of the pubs.

KETTLEWELL – HOME TO AN UNUSUAL FESTIVAL

*T*he charming village of Kettlewell stands to the east of a major crossing point of the river. It is an ancient settlement although the present **St Marys Church** dates only from 1885 when it replaced a previous one that itself had replaced a Norman structure. Today it also provides facilities for worship for the local Methodists and two windows were transferred to it when the Methodist church closed in 1986. The altar window commemorates the battle of the Somme in 1916 and is in memory of the author Godfrey Cutcliffe Hyne who was mortally wounded there and is buried in the churchyard.

Every August there is a week long **Scarecrow Festival** in which organisations, businesses and families build scarecrows, often to a theme. In 1999 it was World Book Year and Pilgrims Progress, All Creatures Great and Small, The Wooden Horse and The Hunchback of Notre Dame were amongst those portrayed. Visitors are invited to complete a Scarecrow Trail and all proceeds go to village charities and causes.

The Blue Bell is a seventeenth-century coaching inn selling John Smith's Bitter and Theakston's Best Bitter through the year with Theakston's XB and Old Peculier in summer and occasionally that company's Mild. It has a large selection of malt whiskies. Food is served at lunchtimes and in the evenings. In winter the pub closes during the afternoons but may remain open if there is a demand. The open fires are certainly an attraction to provide that demand. There is a family room and a garden and also accomodation. (01756 760230)

The Blue Bell Hotel.

The Racehorses.

Opposite is **The Racehorses**, a white rendered, stone built pub that started life as the stable block for Blue Bell opposite. The name is said to derive from 'tracehorses' which were additional horses used to help pull carriages up steep hills. Theakston's beers on sale include Best Bitter, Black Bull and Old Peculier. There is a good selection of food served at lunchtimes and in the evenings in rooms with open fires. There is an attractive garden. Bed and breakfast is available.(01756 760233)

Just off the village centre and backing on to the meandering beck is the **Kings Head** a traditional pub with flagged floors and a large inglenook fireplace with log fires in winter. There is a good selection of beers: Black Sheep Best Bitter, Special and Riggwelter and Tetley Bitter. Food is available at lunchtimes and in the evenings. Walkers are welcome here and the pub is open all day in summer on Fridays, Saturdays and Sundays but closes in the afternoons on other days. The winter hours are variable so it is best to check. There is a pleasant outside drinking area and accomodation is available (01756 760242).

The Kings Head.

About one mile south of Kettlewell on the east side of the river is **Scargill House** a Church of England retreat, holiday and conference centre that can accomodate up to 90 guests. The impressive steeply roofed church was built in 1960. (01756 760234)

LITTONDALE - THE SECRET DALE

*B*efore reaching the overhanging dominance of the limestone outcrop of Kilnsey Crag twin lanes run north-west from the main dale road into beautiful and secretive Littondale, sometimes romantically called Amerdale. Here the River Skirfare takes an nine mile journey from its birthplaces on the high slopes of Pen-y-ghent and Foxup Moor to its joining with the Wharfe. This steep sided dale with valley bottom farms has a true natural, unspoilt beauty. There has been no lead mining here. The villages spill out in line: Hawkswick, Arncliffe - the dale's 'capital' - Litton, Halton Gill, Foxup and Cosh.

At Arncliffe the tidy village green is surrounded by ancient houses, working farms, the towered church of St Oswald, tall trees and of course the village inn, The Falcon, although ironically one interpretation of Arncliffe is Eagles nest. In the church is a commemorative tablet to the many men from Littondale who fought in the battle of Flodden Field in 1513 under Lord Clifford, the Shepherd Lord, who lived at Barden Tower. This battle in Northumberland on the Scottish border was between a large army of the Scots under James IV who was defeated and killed and the smaller English army under Thomas Howard. Earl of Surrey, the commander for Henry VIII. 10,000 out of the 30,000 Scots who fought there were killed. The church has Norman origins but was largely remodelled in 1841 though retaining its fifteenth century tower.

Charles Kingsley spent summers at Bridge House in Arncliffe as well as over the tops at Malham Tarn House and was inspired by the dales to write his fairy tale *The Water Babies*. He set the story in the area calling it Vendale and there are some wonderfully descriptive passages of the countryside in it. His other work included the novels *Westward Ho!* and *Hereward the Wake*. He was Professor of Modern History at Cambridge for nine years and later a canon of Westminster Abbey.

The Falcon Inn also has its literary associations. Halliwell Sutcliffe in his book *The Striding Dales* wrote

> *The Falcon Inn stands as such a tavern should, unobtrusive in its simple dignity with the hospitality of other days.*

This was written more than seventy years ago but it is just as apposite today and it is doubtful if much has changed since those words were penned. It has been in the hands of the Miller family for four generations and is probably the only inn in the dales that still uses gravity to dispense its beers by filling a jug from the stillaged cask of Youngers Scotch Bitter behind the bar and then pouring it into glasses. There are several rooms with flagged floors, open fires and wooden settles with plenty of interest on the walls including many paintings by the

The Falcon Inn at Arncliffe – beer on gravity.

father of present owner. There is bar food at lunchtimes, bed and breakfast is available (01756 770205) and the pub owns four miles of fishing on the River Skirfare. The pub closes in the afternoons reopening at 6.30 pm in summer and 9 pm in winter when it also closes on Thursday evenings.

Arncliffe is serviced by one of the world's least frequent bus services. The 805 Wharfedale Wanderer (Keighley and District Travel 01535 603284) runs on Sundays and Bank Holidays only from the end of May until the end of October. There is one bus from Keighley, Skipton and Ilkley that arrives at 9.55 am and then goes on to Buckden. It returns south leaving Arncliffe at 4.15 pm. Other buses on this service do not turn up the valley. Little changes here thank God. In his *A Dales Sketchbook*, Alfred Wainwright the great writer of walks, has it right: 'Arncliffe,' he says, 'is growing old gracefully.'

Two miles on, passing the nature reserve of Scoska Wood, is the eponymous Litton. Littondale is, as they say in the West Riding, wick with birds. Here you will see redshank, snipe, curlew and plover along with many small birds amongst the ash and rowan trees. The village is smaller than Arncliffe but in the past was important as a ford on the packhorse route to Buckden. A barn by the river was originally the home of the village inn in which the last tenant was a Mrs Taylor. She refused to buy a licence and got away with this by giving away beer to customers who bought slices of parkin from her. A thick twopenny slice deserved a pint, a thin penny piece only a half.

The present village inn, the **Queens Arms**, dates from 1842 although the building is seventeenth century. It has two rooms with oak beams, flagged floors and open fires. It closes during the afternoons except on weekends in the summer. Tetley Bitter is the only cask ale at the moment. Excellent food is served at both lunch times and in the evenings with such treats as rabbit pie and well filled bagettes. There is a garden with superb views and bed and breakfast is available (01756 770208). The owner's dog (Benjamin) is on hand for walks; there is no charge for his services but his popularity is such that it is advisable to book him in advance! The staff, and Benjamin, take a winter break at the end of January.

Queens Arms at Litton – take the owner's dog for a walk

It is possible to take a stiff climb from here over Firth Fell to Buckden and the view from the summit is breathtaking. Otherwise continue up the dale to Halton Gill, a pleasant hamlet with an interesting church which is semi-detached to a cottage. From here a hilly road crosses on the flanks of Pen-y-ghent to Stainforth in Ribblesdale. Half a mile on the road fades out at Foxup but a track will take the curious traveller to the deserted Cosh.

On returning to the main road progress under the shadow of the 140 feet high Kilnsey Crag and watch the daring bravado of the rock climbers. In the fields opposite on the last Tuesday in August is the **Kilnsey Show** during which there is a fell race up and down the crag. Unless you are attending the show this is an area to avoid at that time certainly with a motor car. Across the river in the tiny hamlet of Conistone, where there is no pub, is possibly the oldest church in Craven, **St Mary's**, which has two pre-Norman arches and a Norman font.

On the south side of the rock is the **Tennant Arms** (01756 752301) a seventeenth-century former coaching inn with several letting bedrooms. It sells Black Sheep Best Bitter and Tetley Bitter and serves food at lunch times and in the evenings. The pub closes during the afternoon. There are beams, flagged floors and an open fire in a fine Jacobean fireplace in the main bar. Mastiles Lane, Yorkshire's best-known green road, starts its journey to Malhamdale by the side of the pub. Close by is **Kilnsey Park and Trout Farm** with a conservation centre, pony trekking, nature trail and fly fishing ponds. There is a restaurant and coffee shop and both fresh and smoked trout are on sale along with local game and other goodies. It is open from 9 am to 5.30 pm (dusk in winter) through the year.

GRASSINGTON – CAPITAL OF UPPER WHARFEDALE – FESTIVALS AND A CIRCULAR WALK

On the approaches to Grassington just off the B6160 is the **Long Ashes Inn** in a caravan and mobile home park of the same name. This is an imposing limestone building with stone walls and beamed ceilings. There are five en suite bedrooms to let and the use of the adjacent leisure centre with swimming pool and other health facilities are free to overnight guests (01756 752434). Dogs are welcome. The pub is open all day and food for which there is an homemade emphasis is served at lunchtimes and evenings. Black Sheep Best Bitter and Riggwelter, Theakston Best Bitter and Mild, Taylor Best Bitter and Landlord are the beers on sale together with guest ales in summer. There is a large patio area.

On into Grassington which was a Brigantean settlement in Iron Age times that grew into a medieval market town with a corn mill and a fair. The rich veins of lead ore under Grassington Moor had been mined from Roman times and during the industrial revolution the old town changed to look somewhat as it does today.It has always been the chief town of the upper valley and these days is the principal tourist spot. There is a Tourist Information Centre here and a Yorkshire Dales National Parks Centre.

In the square is the **Upper Wharfedale Folk Museum** housed in two eighteenth-century former lead miners cottages. Exhibits depict the history, life and work of the area and include a relief map of Grassington in the nineteenth century. The village hosts the impressive **Grassington Festival of the Arts** every summer towards the end of June. It lasts two weeks and attracts international patronage with music of all kinds, theatre, exhibitions, films, study days, poetry readings and celebrity speakers. On the first three Saturdays of December the **Grassington Dickensian Festival** is held. It was originally started to boost shopping but has developed into a major event with activities through the day culminating with a torchlight procession and carols in the square. *

A circular walk from Grassington visits Linton church, Linton Falls and the pretty villages of Linton and Threshfield. There are four pubs in Grassington and their pleasures await you at the end of the quite easy four mile walk cum pub crawl.

From the square in Grassington, head southwards down Main Street and on to Station Road. This leads you to the medieval Grassington Bridge, which was rebuilt in 1661 and widened in 1783. The older arches can be still be seen from below. South of the bridge is Lady Well one of the ancient holy wells of Craven. The spring is particularly pure and was for many years Threshfield's most reliable water supply.

Continue on this road to Threshfield in which the **Old Hall Inn** is predominate. It is the oldest inhabited house in Upper Wharfedale - probably fourteenth century – and everything is done in style here. A large bar with flagged floors serves several areas including a newly built conservatory which doubles as a family room. There are open fires and a Yorkshire range. There is also a beer garden with an aviary. It closes on Mondays and in the afternoons. Meals which are served in the bar and the separate dining room are available at all sessions and are of a high quality as its fifth entry in *Good Pub Food* will confirm. (See recipe on page 96.) Real ales from Timothy Taylor's brewery include Golden Best, Best Bitter and Landlord. Two character holiday cottages behind the pub are available to let (01756 752441). The old village was once the centre of the Wharfedale besom (broom) industry and it still retains its stocks on the village green.

From Threshfield head south towards Cracoe until you reach the junction with Moor Lane. Not on this walk but two miles to the south of here on the main Skipton Road in the tiny hamlet of Cracoe is the **Devonshire Arms**. This long low attractive building of white washed stone is the only outlet in the Dales for the Lakeland brewery of Jennings. It has a stone flagged floor in the bar and a pleasant restaurant, both with open fires, and there is an attractive beer garden. The pub remains open all day and food is served at lunchtimes and evenings. The beers include Jennings Bitter and another Jennings beer and Theakston Best Bitter as well as a large selection of single malt whiskies. There are six letting bedrooms (01756 730237).

---

* There is an excellent map and guide to Grassington and district by Aruthur Gemmel, published by Stile Publications of Otley.

Fifty years separate these two pictures of The Old Hall at Threshfield – the oldest
inhabited house in Upper Wharfedale

OLD MARY OF THE FOUNTAINE INN

'It is not many years since an immemorial custom was in vogue at the Fountaine Inn. 'Old Mary', of quiet and pleasant memory was the landlady there, and on each side of the hearth was an oak chair, with a churchwarden pipe on the wall above it. One chair and pipe were appropriated to the Squire of Linton, who lived just beyond what had been Daykins house; the other to Christopher Dean, a yeoman born of yeoman stock whose ancestry went back to Elizabethan days. Whoever chanced to be sitting in one or other of the chairs must yield if its proper tenant entered; and the Squire and Christopher would sit together on many an evening dicussing tomorrows weather or the tales of centuries long dead. Shepherds and farmers – a travelling tinker, maybe, stumping in to join the company – would put in a slow jest now and then. And Mary, with her wrinkled, kindly face, would stand and watch them all. They were guests of her tavern, rather than money bringers; and if her ale was ripe and nutty, so was her outlook upon men and life.'

Linton Three Bridges from
The Striding Dales by Halliwell Sutcliffe

Otherwise just before the Moor Lane junction turn left onto a footpath which takes you over the old railway by a footbridge, on into Linton and the **Fountaine Inn**. Charity often leaves its mark by way of commemorative plaques, statues and sometimes a building but rarely by a public house. This one is named after Richard Fountaine who endowed the impressive almshouses known as **Fountaine's Hospital** at the far end of the green. They were built in 1721 possibly to a design of Vanburgh.

The pub is prominately white painted following a recent extensive refurbishment and stands on the top side of the large village green. Inside it is low beamed with areas divided by high backed settles and warmed in winter by open fires. The ancient pub game of Ring the Bull is played here. It is open all day with food at lunchtimes and evenings and there is a separate restaurant and a no smoking area. Black Sheep Best Bitter, Theakston Best Bitter, Black Bull and Old Peculier, John Smith Bitter, Tetley Bitter and guest beers make up an impressive beer list.

Linton is a picturesque village with some pleasant old buildings and amazingly five river crossings: the road bridge, a pack horse bridge, footbridge, a ford and stepping stones. On leaving the village head eastward towards the charming little **St Michael's Church** which is secluded on a bend in the river and has a fascinating history. It was probably a pagan religious site and it retains some Norman connections.

Turn upstream and cross the river by the footbridge. From the right of the bridge you can view Linton Falls as the river tumbles over limestone steps a result of the Craven Fault. Go up through Snake Walk to join Sedber Lane and Hebden Road, turning left to return to the square in Grassington by passing the National Park Offices. The four watering holes are all on or nearby the market square.

The **Black Horse Hotel** (01756 752770) is in Garrs Lane just off the square. This 200-year-old whitewashed pub hotel is a former coaching inn. It remains residential with 15 bedrooms. There are log fires in the main L-shaped bar with its imposing fireplace and in the dining room. There is a good selection of beers including Theakston Best Bitter and Old Peculiar, Black Sheep Best Bitter and Special, John Smith Bitter, Tetley Bitter and Webster Green Label. Food is served in bar and restaurant at lunchtimes and evenings. Open all day. Fishing permits are issued from here.

Set in the heart of the village on Main Street is the **Foresters Arms**. It is a locals' pub and the headquarters of several local sports clubs but visitors are still very welcome. A single bar serves four distinct areas with Tetley Mild and Bitter, Black Sheep Best Bitter, Special and Riggwelter and Boddington's Bitter. The pub opens all day and food from a single menu is served in both the dining room and the bar at lunchtimes and evenings. It has been in the hands of the same family for more than 25 years. It is residential and pets are welcome.(01756 752349)

On Main Street facing into the square is the **Devonshire Hotel**, a stone built, attractive looking hotel with a large bar, separate dining room and family room. There is a fine collection of Heath Robinson prints. It is open all day with meals available at lunchtimes and in the evenings during the week and all day up to 9 pm at the weekends. There are nine en suite bedrooms (01756 752525). Theakston Best Bitter, XB and Old Peculier and Tetley Bitter are on the handpumps.

The Devonshire Hotel – one of Grassington's fine pubs

The Grassington House Hotel (01756 752406) is a large residential hotel on the top side of the square. The Rose restaurant provides food at both lunchtimes and in the evenings and the public bar styled 'ale house' supplies Black Sheep Best Bitter and Boddington Bitter. There are tables on a large frontage from which to view the passing scene.

Hebden is a quiet village to the east of Grassington that sits astride Hebden Beck, a tributary of the Wharfe, with some small but wonderful waterfalls. The travel writer Arthur Mee said 'Its glory is its setting by a deep wooded glen, where the Hebden Beck comes from a pretty waterfall on its way to the Wharfe.' The Clarendon Hotel is a Victorian pub built of Yorkshire stone with a large open bar, a dining room and an outside drinking area. On sale are Taylor Best Bitter and Tetley Bitter which are joined by Black Sheep Best Bitter in the summer. The meals which are highly rated, particularly steaks, are served at both lunchtimes and in the evenings every day. The pub which has a cricket theme closes in the afternoon.

BURNSALL & APTRICK – TALES OF DICK WHITTINGTON, HIGHWAYMEN AND NO SMOKING PUBS

*A*t Burnsall the **Red Lion** takes its place in one of the most attractive scenes in the dales. The picturesque country inn is in a splendid setting by the handsome bridge at an ox-bow in the river where it broadens and takes a leisurely pace. It is an ancient establishment with origins in the twelfth century although it has been much altered over the years. It claims a ghost that occasionally turns off the beer taps. In the sixteenth century it was called the Ferrymans Inn and presumably serviced a ferry across the Wharfe before the building of the bridge in 1612. Beamed ceilings and oak floors are all part of the character of the inn which opens all day. Beers on sale include Theakston Best Bitter, Black Bull and Old Peculiar, John Smith Bitter and Morland Old Speckled Hen. Meals are served in the bar at all lunchtime and evening sessions and in the classy restaurant every night from 7 pm to 9.30 pm. Walkers are expected to remove boots on entering the pub. The red lion on the sign is the coat of arms of the Harlington family of nearby Harlington Hall.

The parish church of **St Wilfred** dates from 1140 although in 1612 it was 'butified' by Sir William Craven (see Dick Whittington) and completely restored in 1859. Amongst its delights are a unique centrally-pivoted lych-gate, a Norman font, a fifteenth-century alabaster panel that was unearthed in the

Red Lion at Burnsall, formerly called the Ferrymans Inn.

1859 work. The Dawson family tomb contains a crucifix and lettering by Eric Gill.

Burnsall Feast and Fell Races are held on the Saturday in mid-August nearest to the feast of St Wilfred. The fell race is probably the oldest in the dales and certainly the most popular. Its origins are in pre-Elizabethan times and although it went out of fashion for many years it started afresh around 1840. Today there is an open race and others for ladies, juniors, and seniors. Runners in the main race climb Burnsall Fell to a cairn at 1,345 feet and then dash down on a different route. On the same day there are other sporting competitions, a flower festival and all the fun of the fair.

High above and facing the fair green is the imposing **Devonshire Fell Hotel and Bistro** formerly called the Fell Hotel. It has recently undergone a large refurbishment and appears to have changed its style.

This pleasant straggling village of Appletreewick (the farmstead of the apple trees) lies across the valley from Simon's Seat one and a half miles from Burnsall on the Dalesway and a minor road that follows the north-east side of the river parallel to the main valley road. These days Appletreewick, called 'Aptrick' by the locals, is a peaceful place but in former times it was a bustling centre for sheep sales and lead mining. Some fine old houses remain including Low Hall, High Hall and Monks Hall, sometimes called Mock Beggar Hall. There are two pubs, both on the main street and both close during the afternoons.

The New Inn, (01756 720252) is a white rendered stone building with an attractive garden from which there are wonderful views. There is a separate

New Inn at Appletreewick – everybody is welcome

dining room which doubles as a family room in which children are welcome. A sign indicates that hikers, mountain bikers, cyclists and horse riders are welcome. There is a fine selection of beers including John Smith's Bitter, Theakston Black Bull, a beer from the Daleside brewery in Harrogate and a guest ale together with three Belgian beers on draught: Straffe Hendrick, Liefmans Kriek and Frambozen. And there are more than 30 Belgian and foreign bottled beers. Bar meals are served at lunch times and accommodation is available. This is a regular *Good Beer Guide* entry.

One of Yorkshire's most eccentric landlords, John Showers, held court here in the 1960s and 1970s and he created a furore (and lots of publicity for himself and his pub) by banning smoking and proclaiming the pub to be 'England's first licensed smokeless zone'. He wanted to be buried in the garden of the pub in what he called his beloved dales. Sadly, when he died in hospital, his wish was not fulfilled.

The Craven Arms, (01756 720270) is a sturdy seventeenth century limestone house with great views of the dale. Theakston Best Bitter, Black Sheep Best Bitter and Tetley Bitter are on sale all the year round and Black Sheep Special and Riggwelter join them during the summer months. There are good value meals - check out the specials board - both in the bar and in the separate restaurant at lunchtimes and in the evenings. There are two bars

Craven Arms at Appletreewick – log fires and bric-a-brac

SIR WILLIAM CRAVEN - 'DICK WHITTINGTON'

He was born in 1548 at Appletreewick and his family lived in a cottage on the site of the present St John's chapel. At the age of 14 he travelled to London by carrier's cart taking three weeks to do so. He was apprenticed to a city merchant, a mercer, worked hard and gained promotion and eventually married his boss's daughter. In 1610 he became Lord Mayor of London and was knighted. His son married the widowed Queen of Bohemia, the sister of Charles I and was created Earl of Craven. Sir William never forgot his roots and in 1602 built Burnsall Grammar School and ten years later Burnsall Bridge. Later he lived in a house on the site of High Hall. There is no record of him ever owning a cat!

decked out in wood and stone with log fires and loads of bric-a-brac. There is an attractive walled garden.

At the east end of the village a minor road leads through Skyreholme to **Parcevall Hall**. It dates originally from 1535, was extended by the Yorke family in 1671 and turned into a mock Jacobean mansion in 1928 - said then to be the finest house in Upper Wharfedale. It is now an Anglian retreat, holiday and conference centre (01756 720213). The sixteen acres of magnificent gardens are open to the public daily between Easter and October (Admission £2) They contain many unusual shrubs and plants and some wonderful views. History connects the hall with Will Nevison, Swift Nick, the gentleman highwayman, whose ride from Pontefract to York in quick time provided him with an alibi for one of his crimes and is the true tale behind the legend of Dick Turpin. Further on apace is Trollers Ghyll, a strange eerie place in a steep sided ravine with memories of the lead mining industry and reputed to be the lair of the Barguest a phantom dog described as being 'as big as a littlish bear with great eyes like saucers and a shaggy sort o' smell, dragging a clanking chain.'

Parcevall Hall – with 16 acres of magnificent gardens

⑦HE VALE OF BOLTON – THE RIVER'S PRETTIEST STRETCH

⑦he stretch of the river from Barden Tower to Bolton Bridge is probably the prettiest of all. It has received universal praise. Lakeland poet William Wordsworth wrote: 'I recommend to all lovers of beautiful scenery Bolton Abbey and its neighbourhood,' and the American author Nathaniel Hawthorne when describing Bolton Priory said: '...its situation makes its charm. It stands near the River Wharfe - a broad and rapid stream.' But the most telling word portrait comes from the local author Edmund Bogg in his *A Thousand Miles in Wharfedale:*

> *There is not to be found in England a tract of land more beautiful than the vale of Bolton. Rich in fertile meadows, adorned with noble trees and deep, retiring woodland, with long vistas of the brown river hastening through. The ruined Priory and Abbey Church, the ancient gateway surrounded by an amphitheatre of hills enclosing a scene beautiful beyond description, teeming with historic interest.*

And amongst artists who were inspired by it were Turner and Landseer. Bolton Abbey is the name of the village and the estate of the Devonshire family. It includes 75 miles of walks through woodlands and by the river. There are nature trails, tea shops, a restaurant and gift shops. There is plenty of disabled access at several points with electric wheelchairs available free. Car parking costs £3 (£1.50 for orange badge holders) with occupants free. The estate is open all year round.

Barden Tower, a fifteenth-century fortified house, was the hunting lodge of

Barden Tower – once the hunting lodge of the Clifford family

EMBSAY AND BOLTON ABBEY STEAM RAILWAY

The Yorkshire Dales Railway Museum Trust run steam trains on part of a line that originally ran from Skipton to Ilkley via Embsay, Bolton Abbey and Addingham. Work started on the line in 1885 and the first train ran in May, 1888 from Ilkley to Bolton Abbey and in October of that year they were running through to Skipton. It was a busy line and carried many holiday makers and day trippers to Bolton Abbey for Wharfedale and to the spa of Ilkley. The line came under the Beeching axe and it closed in July, 1965. Enthusiasts set up a preservation society with the original intention of running steam trains on the threatened line from Skipton to Grassington but this was rescued as a goods line for quarry working near Cracoe. Activity then switched to the present line and a limited service of passenger trains started in 1973 for a short while although it was not until 1979 that a timetabled service from Embsay to Holywell Halt started. The line was extended eastwards in 1997 through Draughton to Bolton Abbey where the station has been completely rebuilt as a replica of the original. This magnificent piece of work is wonderfully set with a backdrop of Beamsley Beacon and there is a footpath from here to Bolton Abbey village as well as a newly created wetland area that is home to a number of rare plants and flowers. Steam passenger trains operate on the five mile line through the year although the service is limited in winter to Sundays only. There is a daily service through July and August and a number of special events are organised such as Santa trains in December and Friends of Thomas the Tank Engine weekends. There are cafes and gift shops at both stations and occasionally trains have buffet cars with draught beers from the Daleside Brewery.

The railway has a talking timetable on 01756 795189 and general enquiries including requests for copies of the timetable can be made on 01756 710614. There is a web site on: www.yorkshirenet.co.uk/embsaybasteamrailway.

Bolton Abbey Station – rebuilt to its former splendour

the Clifford family and the home of Henry Clifford, the 'Shepherd Lord'. He was brought up as a shepherd boy in Cumberland to keep his identity secret from his father's enemies in War of Roses. He raised an army of local men to fight for the King at Flodden Field and there is a memorial to his men in Arncliffe church. There are tea rooms in the restored priest's house.

The Strid, famed in fact and fable, is where the river reaches its narrowest point surging through a steeply sided gorge and is so named because it appears to be stridable. It isn't, and a goodly number have lost their lives in trying to cross it. The river can be crossed by a castellated footbridge that was once an aqueduct and close by is the Cavendish Pavillion a licensed café and restaurant with a gift shop. Further downstream is another crossing by 57 stepping stones which were laid to allow worshippers easier access to the church.

Bolton Priory (it was never an abbey) is partly ruined but the western end has been restored and the church is still in use. The view from the ruined end is incomparable, John Ruskin referred to it as: '...the sweet peace and tender decay...' The priory dates from 1151 and was supressed in 1539. Restoration work took place between 1875 and 1880 and the present priory church of St Mary and St Cuthbert serves the parish of Bolton Abbey with regular services on Sundays and Wednesdays. **Bolton Hall**, the home of the Devonshire family, is to the west of the main road. It dates from the early fourteenth century and was extended in 1844 to a design by Joseph Paxton. It is not open to the public. In the village there is a tea cottage, a gift shop and a post office.

At Bolton Bridge is the wonderfully sited **Devonshire Arms** a large high class hotel in delightful grounds running down to the river. There is a public bar and brasserie that was refurbished in 1998 with a modern bistro look. The emphasis is on food and wine with meals at lunchtimes and in the evenings up to 10 pm. The bar serves John Smith Bitter, Theakston Best Bitter and Old Peculiar.

$\mathcal{A}$ Pub Crawl of Addingham

$\mathcal{A}$ ddingham is one of the lesser-known treasures of Wharfedale perhaps because for many years it suffered from severe traffic pollution. It is now regaining its inheritance and is a delightful place to visit with some splendid Yorkshire stone houses on the main street, an interesting fifteenth-century church, five unspoilt and traditional pubs and the usual village amenities. The pubs are well spread out in this long straggling village and make a excellent pub crawl with a good choice of beers, first rate food and some interesting historical notes. Halfway down the main street is a well drawn plan of Addingham full of detail and interest.

Buses (service 784 X84) run from Leeds, Otley and Ilkley through Addingham to Skipton and back, hourly for most of the day including Sundays, and there are five stops in the village. The best stop is at the top of the village at the Craven Heifer; it is then an easy downhill walk to the other pubs and there is a bus stop by the Fleece. All the pubs have car parks and outdoor drinking areas.

The Craven Heifer (01943 830106) sells Tetley Mild and Bitter, Black Sheep Best Bitter and Special. It was built in 1820 on the site of a previous pub dating from 1687. The name comes from a gigantic beast born in 1807 and reared at Gargrave by Reverend William Carr incumbent at Bolton. Its height at the shoulder was 5' 2" and length nose to rump 11' 2". It weighed 176 stones 4 lbs. Up to 1817 a picture of it was on notes of the Craven Bank. Several pubs including at least ten in Yorkshire have been named after it and a drawing of the heiffer is in the bar. An L-shaped bar serves a large main room and a restaurant where good quality food is served including such interesting dishes as Louisiana

Craven Heifer at Addingham – named after a gigantic beast.

Catfish with wild rice. The pub closes in the afternoon except on Sundays when it opens all day with meals into the early evening.

The Sailor (01943 830216) was once called the Jolly Sailor and is said to have been a mariners recruitment office (although it is 70 miles from the sea!) It is more than 200 years old although it was largely rebuilt in 1838. It sells Tetley Bitter, Black Sheep Best Bitter and Marston's Pedigree. The bar serves a large comfortable front room and to the left are two pleasant dining rooms where good value meals are served at lunchtimes and evenings until 9.30 pm. Of particular interest is the two course pensioners' lunch on Wednesdays, Thursdays and Fridays which is excellent value at £3.50. There is a most attractive suntrap of a garden at the back of the pub.

At the **Swan Inn** (01943 830375) the beers on sale are Tetley Bitter, Greene King Abbott, Everards Tiger and a guest ale. It was probably built about 1820 but its origins are in the sixteenth century. At the rear is the now derelict one time village mortuary and chapel of rest. The pub has four rooms including a tiny snug, real fires, flagged floors, lots of cricket memorabilia and all the character of a turn of the century inn. The pub food and sandwiches are good and reasonably priced. It is open all day except during weekday afternoons in winter.

In the **Crown Inn** (01943 830274) Theakston Bitter and Tetley Bitter are on sale. This pub was built in 1769 as the datestone above the main door indicates and initially had a brewery behind it. There is a main room containing the bar with two small rooms of great character opening off. There are flagged floors and open fires and a fine brass collection. It is open all day and is very much a locals pub.

The Fleece (01943 830491) has Tetley Mild and Bitter and Ind Coope Draught Burton Ale on the pumps. It was built in 1740 on the site of the village's oldest pub which dated from before 1600. Good value food is served in the bars and in the restaurant both at lunch times and in the evenings. There is jazz on Wednesdays with the generous offer of a free supper, and folk music on Sundays.

The Swan in Addingham – once housed the village mortuary.

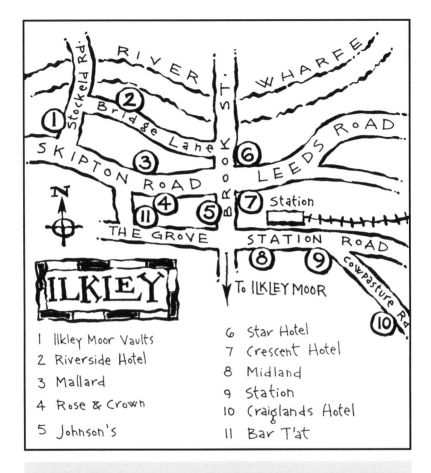

1 Ilkley Moor Vaults	6 Star Hotel
2 Riverside Hotel	7 Crescent Hotel
3 Mallard	8 Midland
4 Rose & Crown	9 Station
5 Johnson's	10 Craiglands Hotel
	11 Bar T'at

BLACK HATS VERSUS WHITE HATS – A CRICKET MATCH AT ILKLEY

A cricket match is still played to this day that was originally started more than 120 years ago to try to get the Ilkley Cricket Club out of debt. In 1880 the tradesmen of the town got together under the enthusiatic leadership of Bill Lister the landlord of the Wharfedale Inn and his friend John Beanlands to play a twenty a side match. It was to become an annual affair. Two years later to add a bit of spice it was decided that one team should wear tall black hats and the other tall white hats.

Changes took place over the years with rosettes replacing hats for a while but hats were back by 1888 and have remained. Entertainment appears to have been the main purpose of the event and for a period only underarm bowling was allowed and batters had to take the opposite stance to their usuual one. Pick shafts and broom handles were used for bats and one of the rules of the match is that excesses of skill and aptitude for the game of cricket will be penalised. Certain references are made to it as the 'tradesmen's' novelty cricket match.

A supper with speeches and entertainment follows the match and this is regarded as a vital part of the day. Prizes go to players for various feats and the winning captain is presented with a silver cup.

The matches ceased with the start of the second world war but commenced again in 1978 on a biennial basis after the cup was discovered in a box at the Manor House museum. A big affair was made of the centenary game in 1980 when it was played on May Day with Yorkshire test cricketers Close and Trueman taking part.

$\mathcal{I}$LKLEY – THE SPA TOWN

$\mathcal{I}$Ikley stands out as one of Yorkshire's most attractive towns particularly because of its wonderful setting below its famous moor which stretches over almost 2,000 acres between Airedale and Wharfedale and is part of the much larger Rombalds Moor. At the moor's north-eastern tip standing guard over the town are the Cow and Calf rocks and across on the western end in Hebers Ghyll is the famous Swastika Stone. Cup and ring stones abound; in fact the whole area teams with mysteries and there are so many different legends to explain them.

The town's origins are in Roman times and the fort of Olicana stood close to the present parish church of All Saints. Up to Victorian times Ilkley was a small village but its growth came about from its development as a spa which led to the building of many hotels and a number of pubs in the 1850s. The arrival of the railway in 1865 from Bradford and Leeds increased its growth and started its popularity as a dormitory town. Ilkley water was merely a cold spring and had no particular mineral content. **White Wells** on the edge of the moor was the first of these cold water baths and dated from around 1760. The patient was submerged in the cold water for as long as possible and then rubbed down with rough towels to induce a wonderful healthy glow. It is still in use today opening at weekends and when a flag flies which is easily visable from the town. Tea and coffee is served made with the spring water.

There have been inns and taverns in Ilkley since the middle ages and the earliest record of one is of Henry Spencer described as a hostilier in the 1379 poll tax returns. The oldest remaining pubs are the Mallard and the Rose and Crown both in Church Street. Today it is disappointing to find that in such an attractive town as Ilkley many of its pubs lack character and some have had what style they had ruined by garish modern alterations and insensitive external advertising. However some are certainly worth a visit.

The **Ilkley Moor Vaults** is in a leafy location on Stockeld Road and is signed from the main A 65 road. It sells Tetley Bitter, Taylor Best Bitter and Landlord and guest beers that are always interesting. It is a two-decker pub that was originally the public bar and the only surviving part of a large hotel which burned down in 1968. There are stone flagged floors and wooden settles and lots of character. Upstairs is a balcony and there is a large outdoor flagged area. Meals are interesting and there is nothing costing more than a fiver. They are served lunchtimes and evenings except Sunday evenings and snacks are available all day.

Nearby in pleasant parkland backing on to the Wharfe is the **Riverside**

Riverside Hotel in Ilkley – boats for hire

Hotel a very attractive hostelry with en suite accommodation and a large play area for children. In the grounds is the Riverside Kabin selling fish and chips, ice cream and hot and cold drinks throughout the year. There are also boats for hire. Cask beers on sale are Thwaites Bitter and Craftsman, Tetley Bitter and Samuel Smith Old Brewery Bitter. It opens at 10 am for coffee and good value meals are available all day up to 8.30 pm in both the bar and dining room of this popular family pub. (01943 607338)

On Church Street are the towns two oldest pubs. **The Mallard** has a date stone of 1709 and it retains its beams, mullioned windows and stonework but its character has almost vanished. It sells John Smith Bitter and does good value food. **The Rose and Crown** opposite Ilkley's splendid parish church is very old but was largely rebuilt in the late Victorian era. It sells Bass beers, meals at lunchtimes and provides accomodation (01943 607338). Around the corner in Brook Street is **Johnson's** a pleasant airy cafe bar on two floors selling Thwaites Bitter and Daniel's Hammer. A range of good value food with a variety of teas and coffees is served from 10 am until 5 pm during the week and from 10 am to 7 pm at weekends .

At the main traffic lights where Brook Street crosses the A 65 stands the Star Hotel with a modern split-level bar with beers from Bass. There is food at lunchtimes and bed and breakfast is available (01535 603301). It was one of the first hotels built to accomodate visitors coming to Ilkley for the waters but was rebuilt in 1905 and of particular note is the splendid clock advertising beers from the long gone Hammond's brewery of Bradford. Opposite is the **Crescent Hotel** (01943 600012) approriately shaped and providing good hotel facilities including 20 en suite bedrooms, a restaurant open in the evenings and a brasserie for food during the day. The busy public bar serves Tetley Bitter,

Theakston Best Bitter and Black Sheep Best Bitter from the handpumps. There is good access for the disabled.

Close to the bus and railway stations is the **Midland Hotel** which dates from 1888 when the railway line was extended to Bolton Abbey. It is open all day and sells John Smith Bitter, Marston Pedigree, Greene King Abbot and guest beers and serves bar food at lunchtimes through the week. There are two bars with wooden settles, open fires, some fine glasswork and pictures of old Ilkley and historic railways. Nearby is the **Station Hotel** a friendly one-bar pub selling Tetley beers and lunches. It also has a collection of railway pictures. Up the hill from here in Cowpasture Road is the well-known **Craiglands Hotel** (01943 607676) with its rather plush bar selling Theakston Best Bitter and Tetley Bitter. Meals and accomodation are its main purpose in life.

Bar t'at – Ilkley's newest pub

Ilkleys newest pub sets out to redress the balance of the rather limited selection of beers available in the town. Excepting the two pubs that sell Thwaites's beers from Lancashire all the others that are regularly available are what might be termed Yorkshire standards. The quirkily titled **Bar t'at** in Cunliffe Road just off The Grove is one of a chain of pubs in the area that aims at an interesting beer menu above all with quality food and wine alongside. It is on two levels connected by a spiral staircase and the lower area is no smoking. The beers on sale include Taylor Landlord, Black Sheep Best Bitter and four others that will vary, along with draught and bottled beers from Belgium and Germany. It has an interesting wine list and a variety of coffees and teas. Good quality bar food is served every lunchtime and in the early evenings from Tuesday to Saturday.

Before leaving the town centre of Ilkley there are two buildings, at least, that deserve a visit. **All Saints parish church** on the north side of the main road is in the perpendicular style built in grey stone with its earliest

All Saints Church, Ilkley – Anglo-Saxon crosses and William Morris glass.

part, the south doorway, dating from the thirteenth century. There is much of interest in the church including three Anglo Saxon crosses, a Jacobean font cover, the fourteenth century effigy of a knight and some stained glass from the William Morris studio.

Close by is the **Manor House Museum** which has its origins in the fifteenth century and is on part of the site of the Roman Fort of Olicana. It is now the town's museum housing local history collections and Roman remains and the art gallery.

Travel east along the A 65 and on the left in splendid isolation is the massive **Wharfedale Gate** a roadhouse with several rooms and a definite food emphasis. It is open all day and sells Boddington Bitter and Whitbread Trophy. Across the road in Ben Rhydding is the **Wheatley Hotel** which has a large L-shaped lounge, a separate dining room and a garden and is open all day. Tetley Bitter is sold. It provides accomodation (01943 607266) and also acts as a village local. Go back to the main road and cross the iron bridge and head for Askwith and the **Black Horse** a former coaching inn high above the river in an attractive setting. It closes in the afternoons during the week but is open all day at weekends. Food in the bar and restaurant are served lunchtimes and evenings from Monday to Saturday and through the day on Sundays until 8 pm. Worthington Bitter is the only cask ale.

ON ILKLA MOOAR BAHT 'AT - THE YORKSHIRE ANTHEM

According to Dr Arnold Kellett author of the book On Ilkla Mooar baht 'at - The Story of the Song the origins of the song are still a matter of romantic legend rather than historical fact. It is set to the music of a hymn tune written by Thomas Clark, a Methodist boot and shoe maker from Canterbury, in 1805. The tune Cranbrook is little used today as a hymn; only occasionally and somewhat light-heartedly for the carol While Shepherds watched their flocks by night. The most popular theory is that it evolved from events that occured during an outing to Ilkley of a glee club or choir from the Calder Valley - Heptonstall is often claimed - possibly on an Easter Monday. But there are dozens of other claimants and other versions.

Wheear 'as ta bin sin ah saw thee,
On Ilkla Moor baht 'at?!
Wheear 'as ta bin sin ah saw thee?
Wheear 'as ta bin sin ah saw thee?
On Ilkla Moor baht 'at?!
On Ilkla Moor baht 'at?!
On Ilkla Moor baht 'at?!

Tha's been a cooartin' Mary Jane
On Ilkla Moor baht 'at

Tha's bahn t'catch thi deeath o'cowd
On Ilkla Moor baht 'at

Then we shall ha' to bury thee
On Ilkla Moor baht 'at

Then t'worms 'll cum and eat thee oop
On Ilkla Moor baht 'at

Then ducks 'll cum and eat oop t'worms
On Ilkla Moor baht 'at

Then we shall go an' ate oop ducks
On Ilkla Moor baht 'at

Then we shall all 'ave etten thee
On Ilkla Moor baht 'at

The last verse is thought to have been added some time later to the original

That's wheer we get us oahn back
On Ilkla Moor baht 'at
That's wheer we get us oahn back
That's wheer we get us oahn back
On Ilkla Moor baht 'at
On Ilkla Moor baht 'at
On Ilkla Moor baht 'at

BURLEY WOODHEAD, MANSTON AND BURLEY IN WHARFEDALE

This group of villages clusters between Ilkley and Otley and is sheltered by Burley Moor and Hawksworth Moor, two of Rombald Moor's children. It is mainly commuterland for Leeds and Bradford but it contains an interesting selection of pubs attracting both locals and visitors.

High up on the south side of the valley in the hamlet of Burley Woodhead is **The Hermit**, a name with a tale that warrants a place of its own in this book. It is a small traditional pub on a fairly busy main road yet out in the sticks under the shadow of Burley Moor and justifiably popular with walkers. There is a pleasant garden. It closes in the afternoon. Meals are served lunchtimes and evenings. On the handpumps are John Smith Bitter and Magnet, Courage Directors and Ruddles Bitter.

The Ebor Way long distance footpath leads into Menston with the first stopping off point at the **Menston Arms** on Main Street, a smart village pub in the Samuel Smith mode with a thatched roof to the bar and lots of brass and ornaments. It closes in the afternoons except on Sundays and serves food every lunchtime apart from Mondays. As one might expect Samuel Smith Old Brewery Bitter is the only cask ale on sale. A little way further on is the **Malt Shovel** a homely old pub with some attractive woodwork and a fine collection of pictures on the walls. There is a children's play area in the garden. The pub closes in the afternoons and serves food at lunchtimes. Tetley Bitter and Stones Best Bitter are on sale.

On the main road through the village (A 65) are two more pubs somewhat different to the first two. The **Hare and Hounds** is a family pub with the emphasis on food and facilities for children - it has a Whacky Warehouse attached and a large garden. It closes on weekday afternoons and food is served for most of the day. Tetley Bitter is on handpump. Further north is **The Fox** a pleasant, large, split-level roadhouse in an attractive situation by a cricket ground. Again there is a food base - meals can be obtained every lunchtime and early evening. Boddington Bitter and Whitbread Trophy are the cask ales available.

Across the main road at the back door to Otley Chevin is the appropriately named **Chevin Inn**. This attractive rural pub stands at a five road cross and on the Ebor Way and affords wonderful views of the dale. Lunches are available but there is no food on Sundays. John Smith Bitter and Courage Directors are the beers on tap. There is a pleasant beer garden and camping facilities.

Like Addingham, Burley in Wharfedale is another village that has restored

The Chevin at Menston – wonderful views of the valley

itself to full bloom after the building of a by-pass. You wonder where the traffic went. Now it is a pleasant walk from one end of the village to the other allowing the heavy goods and speed merchants (or even both) to pollute the A65. All the pubs are on Main Street.

Cutlers Bar and Brasserie, formerly the Malt Shovel, is in a fine Victorian mansion and while it is now a food orientated bar it retains a good selection of cask ales: Tetley Bitter, Worthington Bitter and Morland Old Speckled Hen are the current selection. There is an excellent outdoor area with table service in summer. It opens all day at weekends. There is bar food and the brasserie is open every lunchtime and evening.

Queens Head has a long roadside frontage. The bar walls are decorated with a fascinating selection of pictures of village life in former times. There is no juke box and conversation holds sway. Food is available at lunchtimes and in the evenings and Tetley Bitter and Stones Best Bitter are on tap. There is accomodation (01943 863345).

Red Lion sells Tetley Bitter and occasional guests. It opens all day and food is available lunchtimes and evenings from Tuesday to Saturday and all day on

The Red Lion at Burley – a popular meeting place

Sundays up to 7.30 pm. A stone over the door reads W & W 1893 which probably gives the initials of the builder and the date of construction. It is a village local serving as the meeting place for several clubs: Lions, Round Table, Classic Vehicles Society and a quiz team,

White Horse is a small, completely unspoilt, main road pub with a sunny main bar and a tiny snug which is very popular with domino players. There is

White Horse at Burley – classic pub art.

also a pleasant beer yard. In the main bar there are some fine windows from the former ownership of the now long lost Melbourne Brewery of Leeds. One is original, the other is a copy made after some wanton vandalism. Tetley Mild and Bitter are on sale.

Generous Pioneer a newly built Tom Cobleigh pub at the far western end of the village backing on to the by-pass. It has a family emphasis with a children's play room in separate building, a restaurant selling food all day and a good outside area. Theakston Best Bitter and Black Bull, John Smith Bitter and a guest beer are on sale.

THE HERMIT PUB AT BURLEY WOODHEAD

The pub is named after Job Senior who was born at Ilkley in 1780 and was blessed with the power to sing treble, alto, tenor and bass within the same hymn. He was left a fortune, squandered it on drink and shortly after marrying late in life had the misfortune to lose his wife in a domestic accident, for which he was unjustly blamed. His wife's relatives destroyed his house and stole his savings. He turned hermit and lived at Burley Woodhead on the edge of Rombalds Moor. He became a weather prophet and was thought to possess the power to foretell the future. One day when feeling unwell some youths added spirits to his ale and it made him worse. He developed cholera and lay ill in a barn by the Wheatsheaf Inn on the Ilkley Road. The landlord sent for parish authorities and Job was moved to the workhouse at Carlton where he died at the age of 77 and is buried in the churchyard at Burley-in-Wharfedale.

OTLEY – THE GATEWAY TO WHARFEDALE

This splendid market town has been part of the metropolitan borough of Leeds since 1974 yet it remains a firmly established independent place. It nestles in the Wharfe valley under the shadow of the Chevin, an impressive hill from which there are wonderful views across Wharfedale towards Harrogate. Thomas Chippendale was born here and a handsome statue to Englands greatest cabinet maker stands in Manor Square in the town centre. There is also an interesting monument in the parish churchyard to labourers who died whilst building a nearby railway tunnel.

Brewing was never big business in Otley except in the inns themselves.

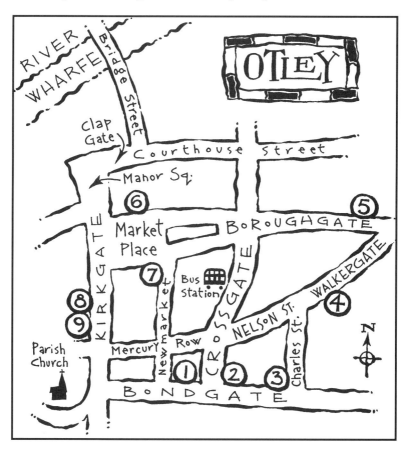

William Kendall is recorded as brewing at Ivy House on Mercury Row in 1800 but the last landlord to brew his own ale was George Robinson at the Cross Pipes in Westgate where the practice ceased in 1910 although he was still noted as landlord there in 1921. However in 1998 Dr Paul Briscoe set up a small brewery in the cellar of his own house and is supplying small quantities of hand-crafted beers to pubs in the immediate area.

There are twenty-one pubs in Otley, mainly quite old, many are listed buildings and everyone of them sells traditional ale. It makes for a good pub crawl but if you are not satisfied at the end of it you can try out most of the rest for only four are outside the town centre. There are good bus services from York, Harrogate, Leeds, Bradford, Skipton, Wetherby and Ilkley and the bus station is as good a place as any to start from.

Turn right into Crossgate and at the top turn right into Bondgate and on the right is the **Bowling Green** (1) an imposing building set back from the road. It is dated 1757 but this relates to its original purpose when it was the town's court house. It later became the assembly rooms where dances, concerts and public meetings took place. It was also used as a school and a chapel and became an inn in 1825. There is a small bar serving a single L-shaped room which is full of assorted paraphernalia which in the words of its character of a landlord, Trevor Wallis, contains a fascinating collection of bric-a-brac and conversation pieces, some of which have to be seen to be believed. It sells Taylor Landlord, Black Sheep Best Bitter and a beer

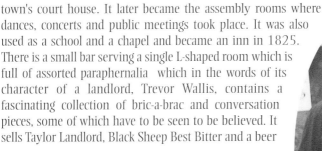

Bowling Green in Otley – 'a fascinating collection of bric-a-brac' so the landlord Trevor Wallis, (right) claims.

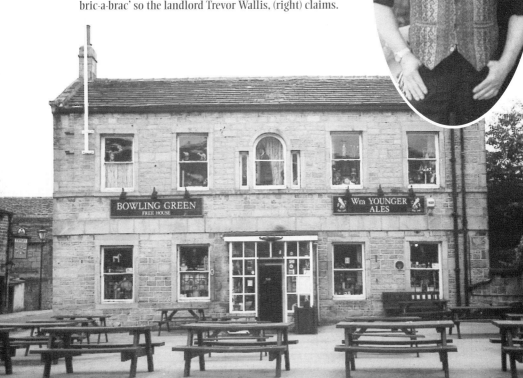

from Briscoe's which is now brewed on the premises. There are facilities for the disabled and plenty of outdoor seating. Food is not served but you can bring in your own so long as it is not fish and chips. The pub closes in the afternoons.

Backtrack along Bondgate to the **Rose and Crown** (2). This one bar pub probably dates back to the seventeenth century but it was substantially altered in 1731 when it was called the Kings Arms with the name changing after the coronation of Queen Victoria in 1837. It sells Boddington Bitter, Tetley Bitter, Castle Eden Ale and guest beers. Food is available at both lunchtimes and in the evenings in the bar and the adjoining restaurant and there are barbecues in summer.

Turn left out of here and you will very soon reach the **Junction** (3) a popular free house that is a regular entry in the *Good Beer Guide*. There is one large bar with tiled floors and some exposed stonework. On sale are a group of regular local beers - Black Sheep Best Bitter, Tetley Bitter, Taylor Golden Best, Best Bitter and Landlord and Theakston Old Peculier - as well as guest beers. Bar food is served at lunchtimes from Monday to Friday. There is a lively atmosphere and it attracts a youngish crowd although oldies like the authors are made most welcome. The pub is open all day. Check out its web site: www.otley.com/junction.

From the Junction turn left and left again into Charles Street and then right to Walkergate for the **Manor House** (4). This terraced pub lies comfortably between shops. It is traditional in every way, unspoilt and welcoming and selling beers from Thwaites of Blackburn. Food is on sale on weekday lunch times and bed and breakfast is available. (01943 463807).

Turn right out of the pub crossing the road and opposite where Walkergate joins Boroughgate is the **White Swan** (5). It dates back to the eighteenth century but apart from the entrance arch most of the pub was rebuilt in the early

The White Swan at Otley – a lively set of regulars

FROM A POSTCARD DEVISED BY DICK SUMNER IN THE 1930'S

Having an hour to spend in Otley the other evening I thought I would have a ramble around the town, and my attention was immediately attracted by a beautiful 'Summer Cross' upon which 'Three Horse Shoes' were nailed, guarded by a 'Red Lion' which stood near a 'Fountain' where a groom named 'George' wearing a 'Blue Bell' in his coat who came from a 'Manor House' called the 'Wharfedale' was giving a 'White Horse', a 'Bay Horse' and a 'Black Horse' a drink; whilst a handsome 'White Swan' 'New Inn' the water was swimming gracefully about.

Turning round I saw a 'Wheatsheaf' standing under the shade of a splendid 'Royal Oak' which sheltered the 'Leeds House'. Hearing a shout I looked up and saw a man who had stolen a 'Rose and Crown' bearing the stamp of the 'Queen's Head' running across the 'Bowling Green' pursued by a crowd of people and a butcher with a 'Black Bull'. He tried to effect a 'Junction' with his mate, a conjurer who was juggling with two 'Cross Pipes' and a 'Cock and Bottle' but failing in his attempt ran straight into the 'Masons Arms' who was coming out of the 'Dramshop' with a heavy 'Woolpack' on his shoulders made from the 'Fleece' of a prize sheep; and with the sound of 'The Ring o' Bells' ringing merrily in my ears, I retired to rest aided by the light of the 'Half Moon' and the evening 'Star'.

years of the last century. However the original stables and the ostler's house remain. The regulars of this thriving pub who are a lively lot have been responsible for raising the money to buy and train many guide dogs for the blind. The White Swan, which is open all day, sells Stones Best Bitter, Black Sheep Best Bitter, John Smith Bitter and occasionally a guest beer. There is a sun trap of a yard at the back. There is no accomodation here but a list of other pubs in the town providing it is displayed.

Take a right turn along Boroughgate passing the bus station on your left. There is no reflection of Otley's most famous son, Thomas Chippendale, amongst the names of its pubs although there was once a Carpenters Arms where the bus station now stands. It stood opposite the house where he was born. It was later named the Wharfedale but was demolished in 1934. Carry on to the **Bay Horse** (6), a gem of a nineteenth-century pub with a welcoming look that comes from winning the Leeds Pub in Bloom competition in 1998 and 1999. It is completely unspoilt retaining its tiny tap room with serving hatch, alcoves in the lounge, a gracefully curving bar, some splendid stained glass and a collection of photographs of old Otley. Beers include Tetley Mild and Bitter, Greene King Abbot and two constantly changing guest beers one of which will be from a local independent brewery occasionally from Briscoe's the Otley micro-brewery. Basic, good value snacks including 'possibly the best beef sandwich in the world' are available until late afternoon. It has a magnificent garden at the back and a passageway from here separated it from the Melbourne Vaults which closed to become two shops. The Vaults as it was popularly known had a rental charged upon it for the benefit of the town's poor.

From here go straight across the Market Place to the **Black Bull** (7). This is a magnificent little-altered tavern which retains an atmosphere reminiscent of medieval times. It may be the oldest pub in Otley although there are other claimants. It is long and low, white-rendered and with a proud sign which, like many others in the immediate area, reflect the rural and agrarian location of the town. The main door to the Black Bull if not original is very old, solid and impressive, whilst inside is a stone fireplace probably dating from its origins along with a beautifully preserved bread oven with its original arched brickwork still intact. In its yard are stables, a water pump and a stone staircase. Much of the present Black Bull is eighteenth-century but there is ample evidence that some parts date from even earlier when it was two buildings. In 1648 a party of Cromwell's Ironsides is said to have called here for refreshment and drunk the tavern dry. Such tales are apocryphal but somehow this one seems quite plausible. Today it sells Taylor Landlord and Best Bitter, Tetley Bitter, and occasional guest beers with big reductions in price during the happy hours of 4 pm to 7 pm on weekdays. The pub is open all day and good value meals are sold at lunchtimes.

Go left through the Market Place and look next door at was once the New Inn, a splendid Victorian pub with excellent stained glass bay windows advertising its one-time owner William Whitaker of Bradford. It closed in 1990 and, as the result of some corporate vandalism, is now insensitively redecorated in the garish colours of a cut price drug store. The windows sadly, have gone and the only memory is an area behind named New Inn Yard.

Turn left by the cross into Kirkgate which at one time was thickly laid with

THOMAS CHIPPENDALE

Thomas Chippendale was born in Otley in 1718 the son of a joiner. He became one of the best-known English furniture and cabinet makers of the eighteenth century and was famous for his book *The Gentleman & Cabinet Maker's Director* which illustrated most styles of domestic furniture of the period. After serving a family apprenticeship he moved to London, married Catherine Redshaw in 1748 and set up a workshop which he later moved to St Martins Lane to the centre of the capital's furniture business. Chippendale formed a partnership first with James Rannie, an upholsterer who died in 1766, and then, in 1771, with Thomas Haig. Chippendale's son, also called Thomas, joined him and eventually succeeded him in the business. It was a large firm in contemporary terms employing more then 50 craftsmen and producing work for many wealthy clients. His work can still be seen in many stately homes including Aske Hall, Nostell Priory, Harewood House, Newby Hall and Burton Constable all in Yorkshire. Chippendale's first wife died in 1772, and he married Elizabeth Davis in 1777. He died of tuberculosis in London in 1779. His son continued the business as Chippendale and Haig until Haig's retirement in 1796 and then he carried on alone. An impressive statue is in Manor Square, Otley.

inns. Across is the **Red Lion** (8) a small well kept pub with three drinking areas and a garden served by one bar. There are occasional happy hours. Beers usually sold are Courage Directors and John Smith Bitter along with a guest. Food is served at lunch times and and through to 6.30 pm and vegetarians are well catered for.

Next door is the **Whitakers Arms** (9), the name reflecting its one-time ownership by a long gone brewery from Bradford. It was once known as the Dramshop and has kept its excellent stone flagged floors. It is open plan albeit in a traditional style The pub sells Tetley Bitter, Marston Pedigree and a guest ale which is likely to be from a Yorkshire brewery. There is a garden at the back and a separate restaurant and good value food is available both at lunch times and in the evenings.

All Saints parish church is 100 yards further on. There are several Norman architectural features and fragments of Anglo-Saxon crosses some dating from the ninth century. Chippendale was baptised here in 1718. Outside in Church Lane is a memorial to labourers who died whilst building the Bramhope railway tunnel on the Leeds and Thirsk railway between 1845 and 1849. It takes the form of a scale replica of the entrance to the tunnel.

The other pubs of Otley

Black Horse, Westgate. Has a datestone of 1901 although there was an much earlier inn here that was the starting point for coaches running between Otley and York by Harewood and Tadcaster. Through an imposing archway there is an excellently preserved stable yard. The pub is now in cafe bar style and opens all day. There is bar food every lunchtime and lunches on Sunday up to 9 pm. The bistro is open from 5.30 pm to 9 pm from Thursday to Sunday. It sells Tetley Bitter and Black Sheep Best Bitter. Accomodation. (01943 461047)

Cross Pipes, Westgate. It vies with the Black Bull as the town's oldest inn and was the last homebrew pub in the town. An unforgivable piece of vandalism to this pub occurred in 1988 when a splendid porcelain sign of crossed pipes above the door was removed. Small two roomed pub selling Mansfield Riding Bitter and a guest beer. Opens all day on Fridays and Saturdays. Lunches every day. Patio. Accomodation. (01943 463227).

Fleece, Westgate.Large open pub with small tap room. Friendly pub which backs on to the river with a beer garden and a childrens play area. Beers sold include Tetley Bitter and Theakston Best Bitter. Lunches are served every day. The pub closes during the afternoon from Monday to Thursday but is open all day from Friday to Sunday. Accomodation. (01943 462636).

Ring O'Bells, New Market Street. Back street pub in open plan with separate games area. Tetley Mild and Bitter and Black Sheep Best Bitter. Has a pin ball machine. Closes during the afternoons from Monday to Thursday.

THE SPITE

In the middle of Queen's Victoria's reign a man from Otley called William Parkinson made a remark that resulted in a pub changing its name more than one hundred years later. High to the north of Otley, half a mile outside its border, is the Spite, a stone-built pub on the end of a short terrace built in 1783. It became a pub in 1852 and was called the Roebuck. The following year two cottages at the other end of the terrace were also licensed and took the name of the Travellers Inn. The relationship between the two pubs appears to have been an hostile one and it came to a head because of Mr Parkinson. He walked up the hill from Otley on most days and always drank in the Travellers until one fateful day when for reasons best known to himself he decided to call at the Roebuck. He stayed for about an hour and then moved on to his usual watering hole. But the landlady of the Travellers had seen him and she bawled him out, telling him to go back to where he had been drinking before. He returned to the Roebuck, somewhat flustered, and made the now famous remark: 'There's nowt but spite and malice up ere.' And from that day on the Roebuck was known as the Spite and the Travellers as the Malice. In 1884 the Travellers closed down but the Spite lived on although its official name was still the Roebuck. In 1980 when new tenants took over they were confused by the fact that signs on the pub showed both names. The magistrates were unhappy too and wanted one name or the other. So, more than a century after Mr Parkinson drank at the Roebuck it was officially named as the Spite.

Royalty, York Gate. Well out of town high on the Chevin with great views over the airport and the dale. Children are well catered for and there is a family room and a large garden. Facilities for the disabled. Open all day with food at all sessions. Tetley Bitter, Black Sheep Bitter, Marston Pedigree and a guest ale.

Spite, Newall Carr Side. A popular pub that has been tastefully modernised retaining open fires and high backed settles in an open plan on two levels that maintains discrete drinking and dining areas. There is no music. It sells Black Sheep and guest beers and has a high reputation for food and serves meals lunch times and evenings. See separate article.

Summer Cross, Pool Road. Pleasant detached house just outside town. Garden drinking area. It sells Black Sheep and John Smith bitters, Everard Tiger and a weekly changing guest ale. Bar food is served up to 9 pm.

Three Horse Shoes, Bridge Street. A popular pub now reborn under its original name after a period as a trendy bar called the Lix. Tetley Mild and Bitter and two guest ales changing weekly. Bar food all day and Sunday lunches. Live music on Fridays and Saturdays. Accomodation. (01943 461222).

Westbourne, Bradford Road. A large Tom Cobleigh pub just out on the west side of town. It opens all day and food is available up to mid evening. Beers include John Smith Bitter and Webster Green Label. Occasional live entertainment.

Woolpack, Bondgate. Has seventeenth century origins and was called the Fox and Hounds and the King's Arms in its time but it has been much altered . Pleasant building set back from main road. Triangular bar serves Draught Bass, Worthington Bitter, Stones Bitter, Black Sheep Best Bitter and guest beers. Accomodation. (01943 462908). Occasionally appears in YTVs Heartbeat as the Black Dog. Meals at lunchtimes and early evenings. Closes during the afternoons from Monday to Friday.

Yeoman, Gay Lane. Previously called the Fountain and still retains windows from Heys the Bradford brewers. Sells beers from Scottish Courage range and serves meals lunch times and evenings. Garden.

Yew Tree, Newall Carr Road. On the north side of Otley bridge, a mile from town. Imposing stone building with lounge and tap room. Tetley Mild and Bitter. Open all day. Food, which includes a childrens menu, is served at lunch times and evenings from Monday to Saturday and on Sunday lunchtimes up to 4 pm. Garden.

RIFFA, POOL AND ARTHINGTON; BRAMHOPE AND ECCUP

This is another series of small commuter and farming villages in the valley bottom between Otley and Harewood and some overlooking the dale from the south side.

The **Hunters Inn** is at Riffa, let nobody tell you otherwise. It is next to Riffa Farm and close to Riffa Beck, Riffa Wood and Riffa Manor. It is half a mile north of Pool Bridge on the Harrogate Road – the A 658. Other guides show it as being in Pool in Wharfedale which is in another county. This former restaurant sells Tetley Bitter, Theakston Best Bitter and up to seven guest beers which are always interesting and include some from local independent breweries. There are real fires in this two level pub with separated areas. The large patio gives wonderful views over the dale. Lunches and snacks are available in this very welcoming pub.

Cross the border bridge into the Leeds metropolitan district for the **Half Moon** at Pool in Wharfedale. Tetley Bitter and Theakston Best Bitter are on sale in this white painted pub which closes in the afternoons. Food is served every lunchtime and every evening except Sundays. It has a stone flagged bar and a plush lounge with oak beams and a log fire in winter. Bed and breakfast is available in en suite rooms (0113 284 2878).

The **White Hart**, further along Main Street close to the junction of the valley

Hunters Inn at Riffa on the Harrogate road – a beer festival of a pub

road and Pool Bank, is a traditional old pub with stone-flagged floors, original beams and open fires. It opens all day from noon and bar food is served up to 9.30 pm. Draught Bass, Worthington Bitter and Stones Best Bitter and occasional guest beers are on sale.

High up the slope of Pool Bank is the **Dyneley Arms**, well-known because of its prominent position at the crossing of the Bradford to Harrogate and Leeds to Otley roads. It is named after the Dyneley family, local landowners from the seventeenth century. Samuel Smith Old Brewery Bitter is on handpumps and bar food is available at most times. The outside decor is quite drab. There is live music on four nights.

Head towards Leeds on the A 660 for Bramhope and after the first right hand bend spot on the left the tiny **Puritan Chapel** that dates from 1649. It is an important historic building with a three-decker pulpit and box pews. It was built by Robert Dyneley and was one of the very few ecclesiastical buildings to be erected during the Commonwealth. Almost next door is the **Forte Post House** (0113 842448) a large four star hotel with banqueting and conference facilities and a health centre. It is a favourite with visiting sports teams. There are 125 bedrooms and meals including bar food are served all day. The Four Seasons bar sells John Smith Bitter.

In Bramhope village centre at The Cross is the **Fox and Hounds** which dispenses Tetley Mild and Bitter and Marston Pedigree. The date stone over the door says 1728 and this was when it was built as a yeoman's house becoming a pub some time later. It has a traditional layout with flagged corridor, bar area and

Fox and Hounds at Bramhope – sports photographs, charities and flagged floors

tap room. The corridor has an amazing collection of old (and a few recent) sporting photographs. A lot of work is done here for charity. The Ella Dent Trophy for golf is named after a former tenant and when played at Headingley golf club in 1999 £1,300 was raised. There is no canned music. Lunches are served from Monday to Saturday. Ramblers are welcome, there is a large beer garden and dogs with their owners are allowed in the tap room.

Head towards Leeds and stop over at **Golden Acre Park**. The car park is on the right opposite the main entrance with a tunnel path under the busy road. It opened in 1932 as a commercial venture but this flopped in 1938. It was bought by Leeds Council in 1945. There are 137 acres of mature woodland and gardens and a substantial lake which is the home of many species of wildfowl. There is an arboretum and a pinetum, a visitor centre and display house, and a coffee house. It is open all year from dawn to dusk.

Nearby on the main road is the **Parkway Hotel** (0113 267 1552) a large 1930s roadhouse and hotel with a fitness centre. There is bar food available most of the day and the restaurant opens in the evening. The bar sells Tetley Bitter.

For walkers the Leeds Country Way and the Dales Way lead to Eccup and the **New Inn**, where they will receive a positive welcome. Families too, for there is a room specially for children. The large lounge has an open fire and some pleasing carved woodwork. It opens all day and good value, interesting food is available lunchtimes and evenings. Tetley Bitter, draught Burton Ale and a guest beer are on the handpumps.

New Inn at Eccup – walkers and families welcome

The Wharfedale at Arthington – good food and live music

Head now for Arthington where the **Wharfedale** sells Tetley Bitter, Black Sheep Best Bitter, Marston Pedigree and Taylor Landlord. This is a large, handsome, free standing, well established road house with a patio, beer garden and a tiny soccer pitch. The large comfortable lounge is broken into separate areas and there is also a restaurant. Bar food is available all day and the restaurant does meals at lunchtimes and in the evenings up to 10 pm except on Sundays when lunch is served from noon until 5 pm. There is live jazz every Sunday evening and occasional jazz dinner dances as well as other live music including Irish traditional. A couple of miles along the Harewood road is **The Nunnery**, a beautiful many-windowed building dating from 1585. It was originally the site of a Cluniac nunnery founded by Peter de Arthington in 1152.

The Nunnery – on the site of a Cluniac nunery.

$\mathcal{H}$AREWOOD – THE ROYAL CONNECTION

$\mathcal{T}$he Harrogate turnpike out of Leeds was served by several inns and in Harewood village towards the end of the eighteenth century there were six. It was an important halt for coaches. Today only the **Harewood Arms** remains and stands opposite the gates to Harewood House. It was built in 1810 as a coaching house and the stabling in the courtyard remains today converted into letting bedrooms. It is a proud member of the estate of the Samuel Smith brewery with comfortable fittings and surroundings, good beer (Samuel Smith Old Brewery Bitter) and good food in both the bar and the excellent restaurant and a happy atmosphere. There is a garden and facilities for the disabled. (Tel: 0113 288 6566).

Within the gates is the parish church of **All Saints** which dates from the late twelfth century although there was a substantial restoration in 1863 by Giles Gilbert Scott. There is an amazing collection of tombs and momuments. The church is isolated and all but surrounded by trees but in former times had been part of a much larger village. Nearby is the remains of **Harewood Castle** which began life during the reign of Stephen between 1135 and 1154. Today although it still stands guard over Wharfedale it is in ruins and not open to the public.

Harewood House was built between 1759 and 1771 by John Carr of York in the classical style and the southern facade was remodelled in 1843 by Sir Charles Barry. The marvellous interiors were designed by Robert Adam. There are works by Gainsborough, Turner, Angelica Kaufman and Reynolds and furniture by Chippendale. The extensive gardens were designed by Lancelot Capability Brown. It is one of the finest houses in Yorkshire and today is the home of the Earl of Harewood a cousin to the Queen and an ancestor of Henry Lascelles who bought the estate in 1755. The house and grounds are open to the public from 10 am until 5 pm from March to October. There is also a bird garden and a childrens adventure playground. (Tel: 0113 288 6265)

Across Harewood Bridge was the Ship Inn which closed in the 1860s after the turnpike charges were dropped and the toll booth closed. It is shown on the first Ordnance Survey map as being on the east side but the building remains today quite clearly on the west side of the road. The toll house was on the Leeds side of the bridge and in 1753 a pitched battle took place between objectors to the turnpike charges and estate workers from the Lascelles estate. Soldiers stationed at Harewood were called in and ten of the rioters were jailed. Shortly afterwards they were sent to Leeds to quell similar riots in the city at the Old King's Arms in Briggate where the magistrates sat.

Harewood Arms Hotel – once there were six inns in the village, now just one

$\mathcal{E}$AST KESWICK, COLLINGHAM AND BARDSEY – COMMUTER VILLAGES

$\mathcal{M}$ost of East Keswick lies just south of the A659 Harewood to Collingham road and is essentially commuterland for Leeds and York with a considerable amount of new housing fitting in well with the established village.

Travellers Rest (01937 572766) is on the main road two miles east of Harewood. It is white faced and substantial with superb views over the valley. This is a roadhouse with an emphasis on food although drinkers are welcome and there is a small snug and a large beer garden. Beers on sale include Black Sheep Special, Tetley Bitter and occasional guests. Bar food is served at lunch times and in the evenings and a la carte meals are available in the Wharfe View restaurant with tea time specials from Monday to Friday until 7.30 pm.

Old Star in the centre of the village is a discrete stone built early nineteenth century pub full of character with beams and a wood buring stove in the tap room and a smart, comfortable lounge. John Smith's Bitter and a constantly changing guest ale are available along with meals at lunch times. Old Star is not a common name for a pub but there are two others nearby at Collingham and Clifford.

Old Star at East Keswick – a wood burning stove and old style comfort.

Duke of Wellington is at the south end of the village's main street. It probably dates from the 1830s following the Duke's period as Prime Minister. He was responsible for legislation that cut the duty on beer in half and his popularity peaked again as it had done after his defeat of Napoleon at Waterloo in 1815. He is named on more pubs than any other historic figure except Nelson. This stone faced pub has a lively tap room, a comfortable lounge and a pleasant dining room which is often used for musical evenings. John Smith Bitter and Tetley Bitter are sold and lunches are served at weekends with evening meals including an Early Bird menu from Tuesday to Saturday. It is open all day at weekends, every evening and lunchtimes from Wednesday to Friday.

Bardsey is the home of the **Bingley Arms** (01937 572462) which is listed in *The Guinness Book of Records* as one of the claimants for the oldest inhabited inn in Britain. There is a complete set of records detailing all the innkeepers and brewers for ten centuries. Samson Ellis (Elys) was the first recorded in 953 AD and his family remained in control until the late eighteenth century. Up until then it had been known as the Priests Inn possibly because of its closeness to the village church or that later it was used as a rest house for priests travelling between Kirkstall Abbey in Leeds and St Mary's Abbey in York. When the Ellis family left in 1780 the landowner, Lord Bingley who lived at nearby Bramham Park, changed the name to the present one. Nothing remains of the original building although a small part in the centre of the present one is said to date from the tenth century and there are still an eighteenth century Dutch oven and

The Bingley Arms at Bardsley – England's oldest inn

two priest holes. Until 1942 the inn had its own brew house but this was destroyed during an ARP exercise. Water for brewing came from a nearby spring and beer was supplied to private houses and farms in an area up to twelve miles away. Today's pub is extremely comfortable with open fires and its restaurant has a high reputation with meals being served at lunch times and in the evenings. In the traditional tap room and attractive lounge Tetley Mild and Bitter and Taylor's Landlord are sold. There is a pretty sun trap of a garden at the back.

The Saxon church of **All Hallows** is close by and worth a visit. William Congreve, the dramatist, was born at Bardsey Grange in 1669 but the family - his father was an army officer - moved to Ireland shortly afterwards and he was educated there. There is no evidence that he had any further contact with Bardsey or Wharfedale and it seems he may have been essentially an urban man. A quote from *The Way of the World* gives him away: 'I nauseate walking: tis a country diversion. I loathe the country.'

On the busy A58 Leeds to Wetherby road at its junction with the A659 road from Otley to Tadcaster is the bustling little village of Collingham a place well supplied with shops and other good facilitities. The parish church of **St Oswald's** dates from Saxon times; it has a perpendicular tower and inside are the substantial remains of two ancient crosses. And the village has three pubs.

The Old Star is on Leeds Road but backs on to Harewood Road and has two substantial car parks. This stone built pub is food oriented with a separate restaurant but there is a choice of cask beers - Boddington's Bitter, Whitbread Trophy and a guest ale. There is a bar billiards table, a much rarer piece of pub furniture than a pool table.

Half Moon opposite the Old Star is a stylish white rendered pub with a superb walled garden and a conservatory opening from its smart, spacious lounge. The tap room is traditional. John Smith Bitter and Theakston Best Bitter are sold and meals are available every lunch time and on weekday evenings.

Barleycorn is on the main road at the east end of the village. It was given a good makeover when taken over by Thwaites of Blackburn in 1997 and now concentrates on food in its comfortable split level lounge. Thwaites Bitter and Chairman's Premium are on sale. It has an attractive garden.

Old Star at Collingham – seek out the bar billards table

Kirkby Overblow, Sicklinghall and Linton

Kirby Overblow is a small commuter village tucked away in the gently sloping countryside between the river and Harrogate. There are quite a few lovely old buildings, **All Saints church** has some medieval touches but is mainly from a late Victorian refurbishment. Some houses date from the seventeenth and eighteenth centuries although there is a very attractive thirties house with a flat roof.

The two pubs fit well into the character of the village. **The Shoulder of Mutton** is a stone built pub covered in flowers in season with a large lounge, a cosy public bar and a fine beer garden. It closes during the afternoons on weekdays. Tetley Bitter, Black Sheep Best Bitter and Taylor Landlord are on the pumps and food is served at all sessions.

The Star and Garter is also stone built with two bars, a small dining room and a inviting garden available for customers to drink Tetley Bitter, Cameron's Bitter and Ind Coope Draught Burton Ale and enjoy a full food menu all through the day.

At Sicklinghall the **Scotts Arms** is a handsome pub in a long straggling village to the west of Wetherby. It dates from the early eighteenth century when it was built by the Scott family. It is now a Chef and Brewer pub and advertises itself as 'Open all day every day eight days a week!' Food is served through the day until 10 pm with a snack menu and chalk boards for a la carte. John Smith Bitter, Theakston Best Bitter and Old Peculiar and a guest beer are on the handpumps.

Scotts Arms at Sicklinghall – open eight days a week!

On the outskirts of Wetherby at Linton is the **Windmill**. It was built in 1314 as a private residence and has been an inn since 1674. Reputedly it is haunted by the ghost of Alice Johnson the daughter of a licensee in late Victorian times. A very old pear tree grows into the side of the pub and their are claims that this may date from just after Waterloo. There are two bars, a dining room and a conservatory. It is a classy pub yet retaining its traditions with antique settles, oak beams and open fires. It open all day at the weekends but closes in the afternoons in the week. Bar food is served in all rooms at lunchtimes and in the restaurant and conservatory in the evenings up to 9pm. There is an earlybird menu up to 7 pm. Beers on sale include John Smith Bitter, Theakston Best Bitter, Marston Pedigree and three guest beers which change weekly. The Linton village scrapbook is kept at the pub.

Windmill at Linton –
not a lot has changed
in half a century

WETHERBY – HALF WAY FROM LONDON TO EDINBURGH

etherby is a pleasant market town through which at one time the Great North Road ran although its elongated market place was aside of the busy traffic heading south or to Scotland. It is exactly half way between London and Edinburgh - 197 miles to each. It has no great buildings - the parish church dates from 1841 and the Town Hall four years later - many were destroyed in the Great Fire of Wetherby in 1723. In his *Tour Thro' the Whole Island of Great Britain* published in 1727 Daniel Defoe described Wetherby as: '...a small town, but being a great thoroughfare to the north, has several good inns, and a very lofty stone bridge over the River Wharfe.'

The 1379 Poll Tax returns showed that there were no innkeepers in Wetherby and just one in nearby Linton. Other towns in the immediate district had several: Tadcaster had five, Sherburn six and Cawood seven. Yet there were seven brewers in the area. It is possible that some Wetherby inns were run by the Knights Hospitaller, and at least one by a farmer.

THE GREAT FIRE OF WETHERBY

The Great Fire of Wetherby occurred on 11th March, 1723 and was caused by tallow boiling over in a chandler's shop. Forty dwelling houses, the Post Office, other properties and stocks of hay were destroyed. The loss was estimated at more than £7,500. About half of the town needed to be rebuilt.

Few people had been insured and consequently many innkeepers took out insurance with the Sun Fire Office. Richard Browne who owned the Angel with its brew house, malt kiln, granaries, stables and coach house had two policies to the value of £1,000. Isabel Wilbore insured the Red Lion, its brew house, malt kiln and stables for £850. And Christopher Lupton, the owner, and William Parker, the tenant, of the Talbot took out separate policies of £500 each: Lupton for the inn, stables and barn and Parker for the 'moveable goods of the inn.

Over the years Wetherby's inns fulfilled many functions including coaching and carrying, banking, venues for political and administrative meetings, social activities and entertainment. It was very dependent on the trade of the Great North Road and most of the town's pubs were on High Street. The town was also well used by cattle drovers. They came from the Scottish fairs to East Anglia and London by the Great North Road using the Fox Inn one mile north of Wetherby and the Drovers Inn at Micklethwaite also known as the Spotted Ox as their overnight stopping places.

Wetherby was important on both the North-South and East-West coach runs. In 1837 the Angel serviced two mail coaches daily on London to Glasgow routes and two on the Hull-York-Manchester run and was a stop on the Highflyer from Leeds through Wetherby to York and Scarborough. There was a daily carrier service from the Swan and Talbot to Leeds. When the railway station opened at Bolton Percy, a coach service operated between there and the Angel. But by 1848 only the east to west coach routes and a twice a day service from Leeds to York which stopped at the Brunswick were operating. By now Wetherby had its own railway station at the north end of the town on the Church Fenton and Harrogate branch of the York and North Midland Railway and every train arriving there was met by an omnibus from the Angel. Carriers continued to operate to the surrounding villages on market days and the Crown was the principal inn for this purpose. Many innkeepers had other trades such as wheelwright, farmer, blacksmith and agricultural machinist and the inns were used for many purposes.

Todays pubs in Wetherby are a lively bunch, very active in all types of social, sporting and charity activities and by taking the route that follows they provide an interesting pub crawl which is not too arduous and with all the pubs close together it is possible to leave out any that you do not fancy.

Start at the **New Inn** in Westgate at the top end of the Market Place. This cosy stone built two-roomer has etched windows and provides lunches to the

Red Lion in High Street.

accompaniment of Tetley Bitter. In the Market Place is the **Black Bull** which is the home of the Wetherby Rugby League Club. The large L-shaped through lounge has a fine stone fireplace and low beams. The beer garden is quite jolly. It does food at lunch times but not on Sundays. John Smith Bitter and Magnet are on the handpulls. There are facilities for the disabled. Across the Market Place is the attractive **Three Legs**, a listed building which sadly does not sell real ale.

On the other hand the **Red Lion** in High Street certainly does with Tetley Bitter, Black Sheep Bitter, Marston's Pedigree and four or five interesting guest ales on tap. This is a Festival Ale House. It is a good traditional pub with a single bar serving varied spaces and it retains a pleasant old fashioned look. Food is served all day.

Opposite is the **George and Dragon** a three roomed pub with one room overlooking the river - 'the only pub in Wetherby with a view' is the claim.

George and Dragon, 'the pub with a view'.

Meals are served lunchtimes and evenings. John Smith and Boddington Bitters are available. It is renowned for charity events and popular with cycle clubs and racing stablelads.

The Crown Inn is on the High Street fronting on to what was once the ever busy Great North Road. It is an attractively stone built pub with good stained glass windows. As coaching disappeared with the advent of the railways pubs serving the short distance carriers thrived. The Crown was one of these, probably the most important in the town. It has a plush lounge to the front and an active tap room with its own darts alley and a good collection of photographs of old Wetherby. The pub, which is open all day, sells Samuel Smith Old Brewery Bitter at the brewery's amazingly low price and bar food is available at lunchtimes from Tuesday to Sunday. There are facilities for the disabled.

Also in the High Street is **The Brunswick** named after the Duke of Brunswick who died fighting on the British side at Waterloo. It is a large comfortable L-shaped pub selling John Smith Bitter and Magnet and weekday lunches. Bed and breakfast is available (01937 582008).

The Angel is one of Wetherby's oldest pubs and is listed as being of architectural importance. It has an L-shaped bar and claims to be 'the only pub in Wetherby that caters for families'. Food is available at lunchtimes and in the early evenings. There is a football machine and many pictures of farm animals. Worthington and John Smith Bitters are on handpumps and the Dutch lager, Grolsch, is also on draught.

Continue into North Street for the **Swan and Talbot.** This is another listed pub and a former posting and coaching inn formed out of two inns - the Swan and the Talbot. It has recently been refurbished. It has a U-shaped bar, a beer garden and provides accommodation (01937 582040). Food is available on lunchtimes and in the evenings in the bar and the restaurant. Beers available are Tetley Bitter, John Smith Bitter and a guest. It was first licensed in 1678

SWAN AND TALBOT

This important Posting Inn on the Great North Road had ample stabling in coaching days from whence departed the carriers to Leeds. There was a soldiers room under the eaves and a malt kiln in which they brewed their own beer. This Inn was first licensed in 1678.

The tour concludes at the **Royal Oak** in North Street. This white painted pub has an open L-shaped interior with a large tree trunk and a stone faced bar. Meals are served on lunchtimes and evenings but not on Sundays. There is a pleasant garden. Facilities are available for the disabled. John Smith Bitter, Tetley Bitter, Theakston Best Bitter and a guest beer are the real ales on tap.

BRAMHAM, CLIFFORD & BOSTON SPA

*B*ramham is now by-passed by the Great North Road (A1) but was originally firmly rooted astride it and served as one of the minor coaching and posting stops. At least two of its original inns have ceased trading although the former Bay Horse remains as a private house now called the Bay House and carrying the original embossed sign. Three other pubs remain in business and stone built houses mainly from the eighteenth and early nineteenth centuries make this an attractive place particularly since the traffic moved away. The parish church of **All Saints** with its Norman tower is on high ground to the east of the village. Parts of it are late twelfth century and there is some remarkable Art Nouveau panelling on the screen and both sides of the chancel.

In the shadow of the busy Great North Road on Tenter Hill is the **White Horse** a basic two roomed local that opens all day. It has a comfortable lounge and a lively tap room and also a small garden at the back. Worthington Bitter and John Smith Bitter are the regular cask beers. Across the Square over what was once the Great North Road is the **Red Lion** (01937 843524) a handsome pub attracting locals, visitors and passers by. There is a plush split level lounge, a separate dining room and a small tap room. Samuel Smith Old Brewery Bitter is on tap and food is served at all sessions. Families will enjoy the attractive garden.

At the top of Main Street is the **Swan**, a gem of a pub, completely unspoilt and essentially an ale house. It is a locals pub but not in a dominating fashion.

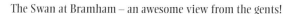

The Swan at Bramham – an awesome view from the gents!

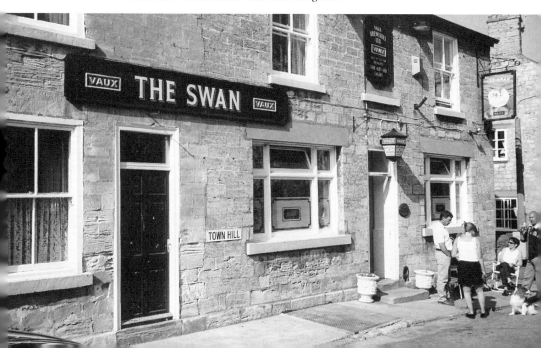

It sells John Smith Bitter. A short passageway leads to the bar and its several offshoot rooms including one which acts as the meeting room for a number of village organisations. The view from the gents is quite spectacular! Apart from weekends the pub does not open until 2 pm and at 5 pm on Wednesdays - known to the locals as 'Black Wednesday'.

To the west of the village and the A1 is **Bramham Park** (01937 844265) a Queen Anne house built between 1698 and 1710 by Lord Bingley a former Lord Mayor of York who became the city's member of parliament and Lord Chamberlain. It contains portraits by Kneller and Reynolds. There are 66 acres of gardens which were built in the manner of Louis XIV at Versailles. The house and gardens are open to the public from mid-June until early September on Sundays, Tuesdays, Wednesdays and Thursdays. The grounds alone are open in the same period on Saturdays and Mondays. The Bramham Three Day Event in mid June is an important date in the equestrian calendar attracting many of the world's greatest riders.

St Edwards Church in Clifford is one of the most unusual Roman Catholic churches in Yorkshire. It was built from 1845 to 1848 by J A Hansom the York architect of Hansom cab fame. The tower which can be seen from miles around was added between1859 and 1866. Money to build the church came from local families, the Pope, the Queen of France and some other minor royals. The statue of the Virgin is by Hoffmann a Roman Jew who changed faiths whilst working on it. Some of the stained glass is by Pugin.

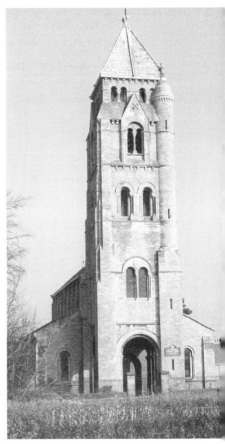

There are two pubs on Clifford's High Street both successfully catering for a local trade while being most welcoming to visitors. The **Old Star** is a well built stone house with a comfortable lounge with a collection of jugs and a smaller room labelled lounge bar where there is an interesting aerial photograph of the village. Samuel Smith Old Brewery Bitter is on handpumps. Further down the street the **Bay Horse** has a traditional layout with the bar serving lounge and tap room with John Smith Bitter and Magnet. Oak beams and a white washed interior give it character. Lunches are served during the week. There is a pleasant garden.

St Edward's RC Church in Clifford – the Pope and the Queen of France helped build it

The Albion at Clifford – a substantial local pub

The Albion is a free standing building a little way out of the village in Chapel Lane on the way to Boston Spa. The large rear lounge and tap room sell John Smith Bitter and the seldom found John Smith Magnet. The pub opens all day and bar food is available every day except Saturday. It is a popular village local but most welcoming to visitors.

The spa of Boston Spa was a mineral spring discovered in 1744 by John Shires of Thorp Arch while cutting wood near the banks of the river. Up into the nineteenth century it was called Thorp Spa. Although the spa has long since gone out of use the village has grown into a small town, very busy and quite upmarket.

The **Crown Hotel** (01937 842608) is on the High Street just west of the town centre. It is stone built with three rooms including one that can be used for conference and other private functions. The beer yard has a petanque piste and sets of boules are available. There is also a children's play area. John Smith Bitter and Marston Pedigree are on sale in the bars which are open all day. Good food is served at lunchtimes and evenings from Monday to Saturday and on Sunday lunchtimes in the bars and the restaurant. There are seven en suite bedrooms to let. The Crown is a popular jazz venue with performances from many well known bands every Saturday evening. For more details try the web site on: www.jazzuk.com/crown

The **Royal Hotel** was built in Georgian times for visitors to the spa. It is on High Street opposite Bridge Road which leads to Thorp Arch. This large hotel with a restaurant attached to it is presently looking rather shabby. John Smith

Bitter and 'an interesting' guest ale are sold. There is accommodation (01937 842142) and a large beer garden.

Admiral Hawke in Boston Spa – the name is full of history

Towards the far east end of the village's main street is the **Admiral Hawke** a pub which dates from the late eighteenth century and takes its name from Admiral Sir Edward Hawke who defeated the French in the battle of Quiberon Bay off the north-west coast of France in 1759 during the Seven Years War. A contemporary record described him as 'the gallant and swift winged victor of Quiberon Bay'. He volunteered for the Royal Navy at the age of fourteen and had a brilliant career. He was well known for the concern he had for the health of his men. In 1776 he was created Lord Hawke, Baron of Towton. Towton, near Tadcaster was the village his mother came from. One of his successors, the seventh Lord Hawke was the autocratic Captain and President of the Yorkshire County Cricket Club at the turn of the nineteenth century. This is a listed building with a pleasant lounge with a tiny snug leading off and a traditional tap room for pub games. It sells Samuel Smith Old Brewery Bitter and there is bar food available at lunchtimes but not at the weekends. The pub is popular with fishermen.

On the edge of the village is the **Fox and Hounds** a straight forward two-roomed village inn selling Samuel Smiths Old Brewery Bitter and sandwiches and light snacks at lunchtimes (except Wednesdays). It closes in the afternoons.

Midway from Boston Spa to Tadcaster is the tiny village of Newton Kyme. You can spot it from the main road by the avenue of trees leading to **Newton Hall** with its pleasing seven-bay colonnade much in the style of southern states American. It was once, along with Nun Appleton Hall, a home of the Fairfax family. The church of **St Andrew** has Norman traces but is mainly fourteenth century.

Across the bridge in Thorp Arch village is the quaintly named **Pax Inn.** Pax is the Latin word for peace and the sign shows a dove - the bird of peace - but as to why it should be used as the name for a pub is a mystery. It is also used as a truce word in childrens games, similar to barley, but this offers no further clues. It is a large free standing stone built pub with a traditional lounge and tap room and its near neighbour is the village cricket ground. John Smith Bitter and a guest ale are sold and bar food is served every lunchtime and every evening except Tuesday. There is a pleasant well equipped outdoor area.

On past the prisons to Walton, a pretty little village and as far east in the Leeds district as it is possible to go. The **Fox and Hounds** is a comfortable village pub next to the cricket field. Good value lunches and evening meals are served and John Smith Bitter and Magnet are on the handpumps. A large circular OS map places Walton in the centre of things. In the village there is a custom of tying strips of cloth to the village well as an offering for cures - water from the Walton rag well was said to cure eye diseases. There is also a folk myth that the highwayman Swift Nick was surprised here by locals who ran away from him thus earning them the name of Walton Calves meaning faint-hearted.

Travel past the massive trading estate and the lending division of the British Library to Wighill and the **White Swan**. This is a delightful unspoilt country pub with its sign in the front garden. There are pleasant outside drinking areas front and rear and a well preserved stable block. Inside there are several rooms and alcoves including a dining room and a traditional tap room. The pub closes in the afternoons. There is food at all sessions with an earlybird menu. Tetley Bitter, Theakston Best Bitter, Draught Bass and John Smith Bitter are the real ales available.

Boston Spa's First Inn

While the bridge between Boston Spa and Thorp Arch was being built a traveller on horseback arrived and took up quarters for the night at the Masons Arms, the first pub in the village. Seeing many workmen about he ordered refreshments to be supplied to them and they enjoyed them selves right gloriously. Elevated by the exhilarating sprit of Old John Barleycorn they loaded their generous benefactor with thanks and having quaffed their liquor, and puffed the fumes of Old Virginian weed to their hearts content, they retired, or rather serpentined each to his home for the night. Next morning, on the ostler going to the stable to look after and dress the travellers horse, lo! to his great surprise and consternation, he found the stable door wide open and the horse gone! Going to the travellers bedroom, to ascertain if he were still there, and tapping gently, but receiving no reply, he opened the door and found - the bird had flown! Instead of paying his reckoning the generous stranger had left on the dressing-table the following epistle:

Dear Boniface,
Obliged by pressure of business to leave your delectable hospitium early this morning, I am sorry I shall not be able at present to settle my small account; but I hope ere long to have an opportunity of doing so. Wishing you, in the meantime, uninterrupted health, and prosperity in your undertaking, at which I thought it my duty, as a pioneering traveller, to be handsome last night.
           I remain, dear Boniface,
           Yours obediently, VIATOR
PS - Don't you wish you may get it, Master Boniface?

For years afterwards the landlord was wont to tell this story to his customers as an excellent joke; always ending with the remark, by way of consolation: 'Niver mind lads! there was luck in the gentlemans letter; for we've niver looked behind us sin that neet.'

From *Lower Wharfedale* by Edmund Bogg.

*T*ADCASTER – BURTON OF THE NORTH

*A*ccepting the fact that Tadcaster is not only the main beer producing town in Yorkshire, but probably also in the north of England, its pubs come as something of a disappointment. For one thing there is very little choice of beers other than the ones brewed in the town. And few of the pubs have any real character. Of the three breweries in Tadcaster only Samuel Smith, a rigidly independent company, have an estate worth preserving. The John Smith brewery is now simply a brewing operation belonging to the Scottish Courage empire although there are several pubs, now owned by non-brewing companies, still signed John Smith and selling the beers. The lack of Bass pubs (there is only

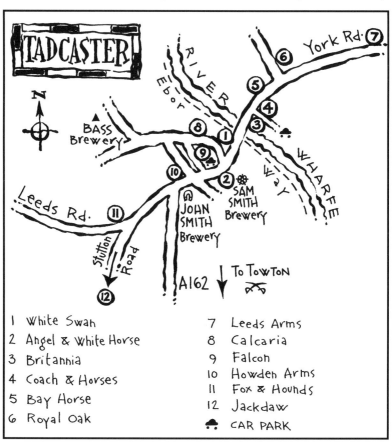

1	White Swan	7	Leeds Arms
2	Angel & White Horse	8	Calcaria
3	Britannia	9	Falcon
4	Coach & Horses	10	Howden Arms
5	Bay Horse	11	Fox & Hounds
6	Royal Oak	12	Jackdaw
		♣	CAR PARK

one) is because the present brewery's predecessor, the Tadcaster Tower Brewery, moved to the town from York and its main estate was in that city.

Nevertheless it is an attractive town sitting astride the River Wharfe close to its tidal reach with its two halves linked by a handsome eighteenth-century bridge. Further upstream is a viaduct built by George Hudson, the Railway King, whose intention it was to construct a direct rail line from York to Leeds. His empire fell and the line was never completed. There is an attractive white stone perpendicular church that in 1875 was carefully taken down and rebuilt five feet higher to protect it from floods. The origins of **St Mary's** were probably in the early part of the eleventh century and it contains some interesting stained glass including the east window which was from the William Morris factory.

The town is dominated by the John Smith brewery with its Italianate chimney, stone faced brewhouse and ornamental ironwork. Another building worth a second glance is The Ark in Kirkgate which dates from the latter half of the fifteenth century. In the eighteenth and nineteenth century it was a pub known as the Old Falcon. Up to 1989 it was a museum of beer and brewing artefacts and local interest displaying a giant sturgeon caught in the Wharfe in 1912. Now it is the offices and council chamber of Tadcaster Town Council as well as a tourist information office (01973 834113).

The town's history starts with the Brigantes and it has been occupied successively by the Romans, Danes, Saxons and Normans. Saxon King Harold moved his troops from Tadcaster in September, 1066 to defeat the invader Harald Hardrada of Norway at Stamford Bridge. Days later after a 250 mile trek south he was to die defending his country against William of Normandy at the Battle of Hastings. History has it that he was killed by an arrow in the eye.

The first account of brewing in Tadcaster was noted in 1341 although in the 1379 poll tax returns there is no record of a brewer in the town but this may be because brewers were often shown as innkeepers. In nearby Wetherby the return showed three brewers.

It was an important coaching centre on the Great North Road run from London to York and the north and on the west-east routes from Lancashire and Leeds to Hull and the coast. At its height more than 50 coaches a day passed through the town. The **White Swan** in Bridge Street is the only remaining coaching inn. Today, although much altered, it is a comfortable town centre pub selling John Smith Bitter and good value lunch time meals.

Opposite is the **Angel and White Horse** which has its origins in two former coaching inns. The Angel was originally called the Red Hart and was built in the early eighteenth century but like many others that depended upon coaching and the post trade it closed as the railway network developed. This was in 1855 and even earlier, in 1841, the White Horse next door had suffered a similar fate. Later the White Horse became the Londesborough Hotel and the Angel was turned into shops. In 1976 the hotel closed down and two years later the new

Angel and White Horse in Tadcaster – a complicated history for a flagship pub

pub, now a flagship for the Samuel Smith brewery, was opened. It is a plush pub with a hotel feel about it. There is some fine wood panelling and furnishings in the large lounge and views into the stables and brewery. It sells Old Brewery Bitter and a fine selection of bottled beers. Meals are served at lunchtimes on weekdays only.

Across the bridge is the **Britannia** with a main bar, a tap room and a dining room serving meals at lunchtimes and in the evenings up to 8 pm. Samuel Smiths Old Brewery Bitter is on tap. It was built as a house in the early 1900s and later became a pub. Licences for fishing the river can be obtained here. On the other side of the car park and bus station is the **Coach and Horses** a popular pub with locals that is open all day selling John Smiths Bitter with bar snacks during the week and good value Sunday lunches. Opposite here is the **Bay Horse** a pleasant traditional old pub selling Samuel Smiths Old Brewery Bitter. It closes in the afternoons and serves pub food on weekday lunchtimes. In the yard there was once a smithy and a Quaker meeting room.

Royal Oak in Wighall Lane at Tadcaster – traditional in every way

The **Royal Oak** in Wighill Lane is a delightful pub with an attractive red brick built exterior, a modern lounge and a public bar that has a separate darts area with own servery. It is traditional in every way being without juke box, pool table and fruit machines. The garden has children's play facilities. Samuel Smith Old Brewery Bitter is on draught. The pub closes during the afternoons. Further out of town on York Road is the free standing **Leeds Arms**. It has a comfortable lounge and a basic bar selling John Smith Bitter and Samuel Smith Old Brewery Bitter. Bar food is served at lunchtimes from Wednesday to Sunday and the pub specialises in buffets.

In the town centre on Westgate is the **Calcaria**, taken from the Roman name of the town. It is two buildings rolled into one and is one of the few pubs in the area that provides bed and breakfast (01943 835965). The only cask ale is John Smith Bitter. It is open all day except on Sundays when it closes from 4.30 pm to 7 pm. Bar food is served weekday and Sunday lunchtimes and Tuesday and Thursday evenings until 7.30 pm. Also in the town centre on Chapel Street by the entrance to the car park in which the weekly market is held is the **Falcon** which is quite old, probably eighteenth century, but is now a cafe bar and restaurant although draught John Smith's Bitter is sold.

Two more Samuel Smith pubs guard the western entrance to the town neither of which were coaching inns although both are quite old. The **Howden**

Arms which is the smallest pub in Tadcaster, is cheekily situated opposite the gates of the John Smith brewery. It is stone built and dates from 1763 with a traditional two room pattern. The **Fox and Hounds** on Leeds Road is a terraced pub with a smart snug and a quiet lounge There is a garden and children are welcome. It suffers from a rather scruffy exterior. The last pub in the town out on Stutton Road is the relatively modern **Jackdaw**, a smart estate pub selling John Smith's bitter.

The railway station at Tadcaster closed in 1965 but it is reasonably well served by coaches and buses. The excellent Coastliners service runs through the day at half hourly intervals linking Leeds with York, Malton and the east coast. Harrogate and District Travel operate services to Boston Spa, Wetherby and Harrogate and several companies run to Stutton, Sherburn in Elmet, Pontefract and Castleford. There is a weekly service to Selby.

THE SMITHS OF TADCASTER

In 1758 John Hartley, the town's postmaster and David Backhouse, landlord of the White Horse, opened a brewery behind the inn in the High Street. It was the forerunner of the present Samuel Smith brewery and remains as the oldest one operating in Yorkshire. The Royal Mail operation in Tadcaster as well as the brewery was run by the Hartley family through four generations and whilst it ran profitably when coaching and posting flourished the coming of the railway changed all that.

By 1847 the brewery was run down and it was then that John Smith, a tanner from Meanwood in Leeds, bought it from Jane Hartley a surviving widow of the postmaster's family. He had two brothers: William who entered the business with John as a partner, and Samuel who remained in the family tanning business in Leeds. Both John and William were bachelors.

The business did well initially under the Smiths but on John's death in 1879 it was once more moving into deterioration. The remaining brothers were not good friends and John's will did not help matters. The brewery building was left to them both in common for their lives but after that it reverted to the sons of Samuel being the only male heirs in the family. The business was left jointly to the brothers but William bought out Samuel's share and when Samuel died in 1880 William refused to take his son, also called Samuel, as a partner when he came of age two years later.

Young Samuel was therefore left with a derelict brewery and his uncle William had started to build a new brewery almost next door at a cost of £130,000. He took with him the business and the trade names and it opened in 1884. Two nephews, sons of his sister, joined him in the venture and, at his request, added the name Smith after their existing name of Riley. Riley-Smiths were directors of the company for many years and it is a name that exists in the town to this day.

When William died in 1886 the nephews had a thriving business. In six years they saw its barrelage rise from 25,000 to 150,000 a year. In 1892 the company was incorporated but the Riley-Smith brothers maintained control. Henry Riley-Smith was the first chairman and remained in the position for twenty years. Meanwhile the young Samuel Smith refurbished the old brewery and in 1886 started brewing again. Today his grandsons are running the brewery.

NORTH OF THE RIVER – ALONG THE YORK ROAD

*T*he old world village of Bolton Percy lies south of the A 64 trunk road after leaving Tadcaster, the sign post is for Oxton. **All Saints Church** was consecrated in 1424 after being built by the Vicar who died the year before. It is a large white stone building with a tower and inside contains a lot of Jacobean work including a full set of box pews. There is some fifteenth-century glass with a complete set of saints and bishops in the east window and another window is from the William Morris works. In the churchyard is an Elizabethan sundial and the cemetery has now been turned into a wildflower garden. **The Crown** is a most attractive pub near to the church. It has two rooms and a pleasant garden with a footbridge over a stream. A pump dated 1801 is at the front of the pub and there is a very old barn adjoining. Only keg beers from Sam Smith's are sold. Nun Appleton Hall and park are about a mile and a half to the east. Its origins are in the late seventeenth century but there have been additions in Victorian times and in the 1920s. It was the home of Thomas Fairfax, one of Cromwells generals, and the poet Andrew Marvell lived here for a while when he was the language tutor to Fairfax's daughter.

Nearby Appleton Roebuck is an attractive village with a green, local shops, churches and pubs. The **Roebuck** in Main Street is a red-brick building delightfully florally decorated in summer. It is a rustic pub with a large bar serving three separate areas some of which are floor tiled. A pool and games room contains an ineresting collection of old bottles, jars and jugs. This is a genuine village local that is big into charity – a community pub of the best sort. There are open fires and a splendid Yorkshire range. Tables are set out in the garden and there is a large pasture for kids to play in. Samuel Smith Old Brewery Bitter is sold. Food is served lunch times and evenings from Tuesday to Saturday

The appropriately named Roebuck Inn at Appleton Roebuck.

Ye Old Sun Inn at Colton – gardens for those days in the Sun.

and there is also a traditional Sunday lunch. The pub closes during the afternoons.

On Chapel Green is the **Shoulder of Mutton** another typical two-roomed Samuel Smith pub selling Old Brewery Bitter. This is a smart cream rendered village local, well proportioned with an unobtrusive addition. The front garden is seasonably full of flowers. The bar lounge is quite plush and there is a collection of long case clocks. Reasonably priced food is served lunchtimes and evenings all week in both the bar and the restaurant. The pub closes in the afternoon.

Returning towards the main road and in the village of Colton is **Ye Old Sun Inn.** This is a well established village pub with a good food trade, in fact two areas are set out for meals. There are bar lunches and evening meals seven days a week. Draught Bass is on the handpumps. There is a large garden to the front and right side.

> **Meanwhile the mind from pleasure less,**
> **Withdraws into its happiness,**
> **Annihilating all that's made**
> **To a green thought in a green shade.**
> *The Garden*

Andrew Marvell, (1621-1678), English poet and satirist, was one of the Metaphysical poets. He was born at Winestead in the East Riding of Yorkshire, and educated at the University of Cambridge. While language tutor to Mary, the daughter of Lord Thomas Fairfax, he lived at Nun Appleton Hall in Lower Wharfedale and wrote the well-known lyric works *The Garden, To His Coy Mistress, The Definition of Love,* and *Bermudas.* From 1659 until his death, Marvell represented Hull in Parliament and his letters to constituents reveal much about his times. In his own day, Marvell was virtually unknown as a lyric poet but renowned as a satirist and patriot. Marvell's prose satire, little read today, was once considered wittier than his verse. His reputation has grown as critics have discovered Marvell's beautiful lyric verse.

$\mathcal{A}$ Pub Crawl Around The Battlefield of Towton

Shakespeare · Third part of Henry VI · Act II · Scene II · Outside the gates of York

Enter a messenger

Messenger. Royal Commanders, be in readiness:

           For with a band of thirty thousand men

           Comes Warwick, backing of the Duke of York;

$\mathcal{I}$n the Wars of the Roses between the army of Henry VI of the House of Lancaster and the Yorkist army of Edward IV the battle of Towton on Palm Sunday, 1461 was said to be the bloodiest ever fought on British soil. Estimates are that more than 75,000 took part and 28,000 died in the battle which lasted ten hours and was fought in blinding snow. It resulted in an overwhelming Yorkist victory despite a deficiency in numbers and Henry fled to Scotland. Three months later Edward was crowned King but the war continued for another five years. Two excellent pamphlets and maps which describe the battle and direct the reader on walks around the battlefield are highly recommended. They are *The Battle of Towton* by Graham Hudson which may now be out of print and the recently revised *Battle of Towton* published by the Towton Battlefield Society (£3). The walk that follows is based on both these walks with occasional deviations.

    The walk around the battlefield takes in lots of history and also visits four good pubs. We start at the **Rockingham Arms** on the A162 road that leads

The Rockingham Arms in Towton – 'probably the best fish and chips in the world'.

south out of Tadcaster. Walk down the bridleway on the north side of the pub; this is the Old London Road and once led to Tadcaster. Go as far as the footbridge over Cock Beck. This was where the final scenes of the battle took place and the Lancastrians were routed. The valley was flooded and the stream was in full flow. The retreating troops piled up and many, unable to cross, drowned, others were slaughtered. Where the smaller river entered the Wharfe it was said to have ran red with blood.

Turn back to the pub and walk down the village main street. In 1996 a grave containing 37 bodies was discovered at Towton Hall on the south-west side of the village. They had been stripped naked and the evidence was that most or all of them had suffered severe head wounds. Historians and archeologists are still trying to discover what was the real story behind this terrible carnage. On Chapel Hill behind Towton Hall was the site of a chapel built by Richard III to the memory of the many who died and were buried there. It is long gone.

Continue past the minor road (B1217) to Saxton. You are skirting the battlefield here and turn on to a signed footpath to Saxton. Now you are walking behind the main Yorkist lines and the path takes you directly into the village. In the graveyard of **All Saints Church** is the altar tomb of Lord Dacre, one of the Lancastrian leaders killed in the battle, who is thought to have been buried upright alongside his horse. The bones of many other soldiers from both armies are also buried here. In Saxton village there are two pubs: the **Greyhound** next to the church and the **Plough** at the south end of the main street.

The Greyhound at Saxton – flagged floors and beer from the wood.

LOTHERTON HALL

There has been a building on site since the seventh century. The Gasgoinge family took over the land in the 1540s and the hall in 1825. It was extended and remodelled from 1893 when Col Frederick Gasgoinge inherited it. The estate was left to Sir Alvary Gasgoinge in 1937 and he lived there from 1953 and presented the house to Leeds City Council in 1968 with the park, gardens and art collections. It contains an important costume collection and furniture, paintings and ceramics. There is a local artists gallery. In the grounds is a bird garden and red and fallow deer. The estate is open from Tuesdays to Saturdays from 10am to 5pm and on Sundays from 1pm to 5pm. (4pm Nov /Dec /Mar) The house is closed in January and February. Admission to the house is £2 for adults with £1 for concessions and 50p for children with adults. The Stables Cafe does refreshments and light meals.

Between the two pubs a footpath goes west through a private garden (there is a right of way) and across fields to the **Crooked Billet** on the road to Lotherton Hall (B1217). This pub is also a suitable place to start the battefield walk. However before continuing cross to the centre of the field opposite for a little incidental history. The tiny fourteenth-century chapel of St Mary is widely known as **Lead Church** and was once the private chapel of Lead Hall. It has a three-decker pulpit and was restored by ramblers in 1931 and a service is held each year organised by the Ramblers Association. Despite its age and position there is no known link with the battle of Towton.

Leave the field by the stile at the top left-hand corner and follow the track to its junction with Newstead Lane where you turn right. You are back in the battlefield. At the end of the lane and after crossing Cock Beck you turn left on to the B1217. Walk up to the highest point of the road from where most of the

Lead Church – the rambler's church with a triple deck pulpit

battlefield can be seen. Further on is what is often called Lord Dacre's cross but which in reality has no connection with him for he was killed by an arrow some half mile away in North Acres. The head of the cross is more likely a relic from the lost chapel near Towton Hall. The track from the cross leads towards the right wing of the Lancastrian position. This is a private road but the owner has kindly agreed access to those walking the battlefield. Stop at the gate and return to the road and then proceed into Towton.

The so-called Towton Rose which was really a burnet or Scotch rose, was white with a red centre, grew on the battlefield at one time. It was said to be tinged with blood. There are recent claims that it has been seen again in the area.

The **Rockingham Arms** on the main road at Towton is a long single room pub with small games annexe leading off that contains an unusual circular pool table and in which the ancient game of Merrils is played. There is a guarantee of well kept beer here for the licensee invented a device to keep beer cool in the lines during periods when the pub is closed. It sells Tetley, John Smith and Worthington Bitters. Food is served at all sessions with a particular emphasis on excellent fish and chips - 'probably the best fish and chips in the world' is the claim. Meals are served lunchtimes and evenings from Monday to Saturday and all day on Sunday. The pub, which closes closes in the afternoons during the week, contains some interesting material on the Battle of Towton and is involved in several charity organisations including the Towton illuminations.

The Greyhound in the centre of Saxton next to the church is an ancient establishment and totally unspoilt. It goes without saying that it is a listed building and there would be an uproar from many parts of the nation if any attempt were made to alter its character. The small main bar serves Samuel Smith Old Brewery Bitter from barrels racked behind it and an open fire increases the cosiness factor in winter. Seating includes the stairs and the windowledge. Next to this and divided by a wood partition is a snug cum lounge which doubles as a meeting place for village societies and at the other end of the building is the barless tap room with an fine selection of pub games including bar skittles. Tables outside are well used in summer. Somehow the lack of food here doesn't seem important. Many locals remember the Greyhound when it was thatched.

The Plough at the other end of Saxton's main street is a welcoming pub with a restaurant that is listed by Egon Ronay. Lunches and evening meals until 10 pm are served as well as bar food. Theakston's ales are on sale. The pub is closed all day Monday.

The Crooked Billet at Lead near Saxton is a free standing roadhouse on the road from Towton to Lotherton Hall and it stands opposite the unusual Lead church. There is food at all sessions with its speciality of 'Giant Yorkshire Pudding'. John Smith Bitter is sold. There are two rooms and a conservatory and the pub closes in the afternoons.

BARKSTON ASH, CHURCH FENTON, ULLESKELF AND RYTHER

This group of villages stretching from the Tadcaster to Sherburn road up to the river contain some ancient churches and many other fine buildings including some of the local inns and public houses.

The Barkston Ash was a tree that grew at the reputed centre of the three ridings of Yorkshire. For many years it gave its name to a parliamentary constituency despite the fact that it was probably the smallest village in it. The **Ash Tree** dates from before 1769 and is a main road (A 162) pub with a large, plush, open bar with beamed ceilings with distinct drinking areas. There are open fires, a fine collection of whisky jugs and other collectibles including pictures and prints. Theakston Best Bitter and XB, John Smith Bitter and Black Sheep Best Bitter are on sale. Bar food is served and the separate restaurant is open both at lunchtimes and in the evenings up to 9.30 pm. The interesting wine list contains very little over £10. The pub closes during the afternoons. There is a large well kept beer garden - which is not a playground!. Famous visitors have included Dick Turpin and Winston Churchill.

In the village is **The Boot and Shoe** which is a very active local pub selling Tetley Bitter in its small comfortable lounge with an open fire and basic but friendly bar. There is a pleasant beer garden. The pub closes in the afternoons and serves bar food at every session - a pensioners lunch is available on Mondays and Thursdays for £2.50.

The Ash Tree at Barkston Ash, the centre of the Ridings

Fenton Flyer in Church Fenton – a favourite with Spitfire pilots.

Carry on eastwards to Church Fenton and cross over the railway to the **Junction Hotel** by the station which sells Draught Bass and Stones Best Bitter. It has a games room and serves bar food at lunchtimes during the week. In the centre of the village is the **White Horse** which sells John Smith Bitter. It is a white washed village pub with an open fire, oak beams, a family room and a garden. There are meals at all sessions. Bed and breakfast is available (01937 817243).

All Saints Church has traces of Early English design although there were substantial alterations in the fifteenth century. There is an interesting effigy of a lady with a lion and a demon fighting over a cat.

And at the far east end of the village is the **Fenton Flyer** which sells Mansfield Bitter and Riding Bitter. There are bar meals daily and full Sunday lunches. In the beer garden is a Petanque court and boules may be hired. The Fenton Flyer was a Spitfire from the nearby Royal Air Force station for which this pub was the local. Before the air base came it had been called the New Inn since 1842 and prior to that had been a farm. There are photos of many of the crews that flew from RAF Church Fenton and a list of all the squadrons that have been stationed there.

Go north to Ulleskelf and the **Ulleskelf Arms** which sells Barnsley Bitter, John Smith Bitter, Black Sheep Best Bitter, Taylor Landlord and a guest beer. The pub does good value bed and breakfast and also breakfasts for fishermen – this is at the tidal limit of the river. The pub closes in the afternoons. There are bar meals at lunchtimes and in the evenings and there is also a restaurant and a take out food facility. The beer garden leads to the railway station where stopping trains are few. Families are welcome and there are regular live music sessions.

Nearby is **Grimston Park** with its house built in 1840 by Decimus Burton for the second Lord Howden and his wife who was a Russian princess. The gardens are in a formal Italian style and while the house is now multi-occupied the grounds are often used for equestrian events. Within the park is the tiny hamlet of Kirkby Wharf and the handsome **St Johns Church**. Its external appearance is Victorian from a major restoration in 1860 but the south doorway dates from twelfth century and the door from the seventeenth. The chancel windows are from around 1300.

Another church worth a visit is **All Saints** at Ryther. Its beginnings are either late Saxon or Norman and it contains an interesting group of monuments including tombs of the Ryther family from which the village takes its name. There are two spellings and occasionally Rythre appears. **The Ryther Arms** sells John Smith Bitter and Tetley Bitter. It is an old stone pub that has been renovated sensitively. There are open fires and a good degree of comfort. It only opens from 6 pm and does bar food up to 7.30 pm from Sunday to Thursday and restaurant meals all week up to 10 pm.

St John's church in Kirkby Wharfe – restored but retaining a twelfth-century doorway

*L*AST ORDERS – CAWOOD – WHERE THE WHARFE JOINS THE OUSE

*C*awood is the final call on the 69 miles long meanderings of the River Wharfe. Here at Wharfe's Mouth it meets the Ouse which in turn joins the Humber in its flow to the North Sea. Cawood is rich in history with both regal and religious connections. The Romans had a camp here, the Archbishops of York were resident here for several centuries and Edward I held court at Cawood for five years. Cardinal Wolsey was arrested here for high treason in 1530. He set off on November 6th for his trial in London but died three weeks later at Leicester Abbey. All that is left of the Archbishops castle is the splendid gatehouse. All Saints Church is a little way out of the village on the banks of the Ouse. It is mainly Norman although the tower is perpendicular. There is a bust of George Mountain the son of a local farmer who rose through the church

**The Ferry Inn at Cawood is actually on
The Ouse but Wharfe's Mouth is nearby**

hierarchy to become Archbishop of York but who died on the day after his enthronement.

There was a time when Cawood had 22 pubs, but now only four remain open. They can be visited on a circular walk which also takes in some of the historic sites. A leaflet outlining the walk can be obtained at the post office.

The Jolly Sailor in the Market Place sells John Smith Bitter, Tetley Bitter, Theakston Best Bitter, Rudgate Viking and either Theakston or Highgate Mild. It is the only pub in the area to open all day. There is a large, bustling and friendly front bar with a corridor drinking area. Bar food is available both at lunchtime and in the evening but not Sunday evening.

In King Street backing on to the River Ouse is The Ferry which has an interesting beer list including Adnams Bitter, Mansfield Bitter and Riding Bitter, Taylor Landlord and guests. It is a sixteenth-century inn of great character. There is a wood burning stove in the main bar and oak beams and there are several smaller rooms and a riverside terrace. Food of excellent quality is served at all opening sessions and the pub merits an entry in *Good Pub Food*. It is open all day at weekends and closes at lunchtimes on Mondays and Tuesdays. Bed and breakfast is available (01757 268515).

The Castle in Wistowgate is a handsome brick built pub just off the village centre close to the castle garth. It closes in the afternoons and serves meals at lunchtimes and in the evening up to 9.30 pm. John Smith Bitter and a guest ale are on sale in its two comfortable rooms. On the Sherburn road is the Bay Horse which, at the time of writing, was up for sale. It has a friendly atmosphere in its three rooms which include a tiny snug. Beers include Tetley Bitter and an occasional guest.

THE GREAT FEAST OF CAWOOD

On the 15th January, 1566 1,000 cooks and 1,000 waiters were employed to provide the Great Feast of Cawood to celebrate George Neville's enthronement as Archbishop of York. It was one of the largest banquets ever to be recorded in England. The guests (not recorded except as thousands) ate 500 partridges, 400 mallards and teales, 2,000 geese, 400 woodcocks, 400 plovers, 2,000 chickens, 104 peacocks, 100 dozen quayles, 200 pheasants, 4,000 conies, 608 pykes and bream, 104 oxen, 304 neals, 1,000 muttons, 12 porpoises and seals, 6 wild bulls, 500 stags, bucks and roes, 4,000 pasties of cold venison, 304 yorkes, 1,000 capons, 300 quarters of wheat. This was washed down with 300 tuns of ale, 100 tuns of wine and a pipe (105gallons) of hippocras. And to follow were 9,000 jellies, baked tarts and custards.

THE WHARFE – A RIVER FOR ANGLERS

> Downwards it fleeted ever, and bore its thoughts floating on its oily stream; and the great trout, with their yellow sides and peacock backs, lounged among the eddies, and the silver grayling dimpled and wandered upon the shallows, and the may flies flickered and rustled round him like water fairies, with their green gauzy wings; the coot clanked musically among the reeds; the frogs hummed their ceaseless vesper-monotone; the kingfisher darted from his hole in the bank like a blue spark of electric light; the swallows' bills snapped as they twined and hawked above the pool; the swifts wings' whirred like musket-balls, as they rushed screaming past his head; and ever the river fleeted by, bearing his eyes away down the current, till its wide eddies began to glow with crimson beneath the setting sun.
>
> *Charles Kingsley*

The Wharfe in its upper reaches flows through limestone and the water is very rich and clear with trout and grayling abounding. It is probably the most famous grayling river in Yorkshire. Between Kettlewell and Bolton Abbey the river contains mainly trout and grayling and a few dace. Near to Bolton Abbey it flows through a gorge known as the Strid - it is deceptively narrow and deep as it forces its way between two outcrops of rock. From here to Pool in Wharfedale coarse fish become more numerous although there are still plenty of trout. Dace and chub are abundant around Otley and below Harewood perch, barbel and roach appear together with some pike. Below Wetherby the Wharfe is predominately a coarse fishery but grayling can still be found down to Boston Spa. At Ulleskelf it is tidal and swarms with eels. Bream also put in an appearance and a few flounders are caught.

The Wharfe at Boston Spa – chub and barbel give great sport.

WHERE TO FISH IN AND AROUND WHARFEDALE

The River Skirfare in Littondale

This is a tributary of the Wharfe with shallow glides and pools. Trout and Grayling are caught on wet fly tackle. Information and permits can be obtained from the Falcon Inn in Arncliffe.

River Wharfe from Grassington to Appletrewick

There are several stretches of day ticket waters along this length of the river. Barden, Burnsall and Appletreewick Angling Club own a stretch and Bradford City Angling Association control another. Each section is clearly signposted and tickets and information can be obtained from the tackle shop at 9 Water Street in Skipton, and the Black Lion Hotel in Grassington. The river here alternates between wide shallow glides and deep pools and the river bed is gravel and hard bedrock. Brown trout and grayling are the quarry which run to a good size. Much of this stretch is fly fishing only and traditional wet fly will catch both trout and grayling. On the Bradford length bait fishing is permitted.

River Wharfe at Bolton Abbey

The Bolton Abbey Estate controls five miles of fishing from Barden Bridge to Bolton Bridge on both banks.The fishing is for trout and grayling and is fly fishing only. The river at Bolton Abbey is particularly beautiful, especially in autumn when grayling fishing is at its best. Wet fly is the key to success here. Permits must be obtained in advance from the Estate Office, Bolton Abbey.

River Wharfe at Otley

Otley Anglers control this stretch from 600 yards upsteam of the road bridge to the entry of the River Washburn. Day tickets are not available.

Resevoirs in the Washburn Valley

Fewston is a 156 acre reservoir stocked with trout. Only bank fishing with fly is permitted.

Swinsty is almost the same size as Fewston and the same rules apply.

Thruscross to the north of the A 59 has 142 acres of water and is much deeper than the other two. Bait fishing is allowed here.

Permits for all the reservoirs are available from the vending machine at Swinsty Moor Plantation Office. Fishing is not allowed at Lindley Wood reservoir.

Knotford Lagoons

These are two large still waters adjacent to the river between Otley and Pool in Wharfedale. Leeds Amalgamation control one and Bradford City Anglers the other. Obtain tickets from the tackle shop in Otley or from tackle shops in the two cities. Bream, tench, roach and carp can be caught by all methods. This is also a good area for bird watching.

River Wharfe at Pool in Wharfedale

This fishery is controlled by Leeds Amalgamation and extends for five miles from the River Washburn to Castley Beck, and a further mile and a half below Arthington Viaduct on the left hand bank.Fishing is for trout and coarse fish. No wading is allowed between 25th March and 31st May to protect spawning coarse fish. Bait or fly fishing is allowed and good catches of dace and chub may be had. Trotting with maggot or caster is the most successful method. Permits and day tickets are obtained from Main Street Stores, Pool in Wharfedale or any tackle shop in Leeds.

River Wharfe at Wetherby

This stretch consists of two miles of river controlled by Wetherby Angling Club.The fishing extends from the weir near the town road bridge upstream to Linton Bridge.The stretch contains dace, grayling, barbel, chub and roach with some sizeable pike. There are no restrictions on bait or tackle. Most dace are taken on stick float with maggot and barbel fall to ledgered caster and hemp. Maps showing the extent of the fishing and approach routes can be found outside the George and Dragon public house in Wetherby. Permits and day tickets are available from the George and Dragon and the petrol station in Collingham.

River Wharfe at Boston Spa

Boston Anglers control this stretch from the weir to Newton Kyme. Coarse fish appear in greater numbers here and the chub and barbel give great sport. Maggot and caster produce good bags but the larger fish fall to ledgered meat. Permits and day tickets are available at the Wharfedale Anglers, Main Street, Boston Spa.

River Wharfe at Tadcaster

From upstream at Easedike to downstream of the town Leeds Amalgamation control the fishing rights. Some stretches are day ticket water with information and permits obtainable from all tackle shops in Leeds or the Britannia pub next to Tadcaster's bus station. Chub, barbel, dace, perch and bream are plentiful. Large pike also put in an appearance here. Tidal influence brings the occasional flounder.

River Wharfe at Ulleskelf

Leeds Amalgamation have the rights to this length of river. Bream and roach are the most common fish with flounders and eels showing regularly. Maggot, caster and worm should catch here. Permits from all Leeds tackle shops and from the Ulleskelf Arms by Ulleskelf station. A fine fisherman's breakfast can be had at this pub.

GOLF IN WHARFEDALE

*W*harfedale and its environs is an area that contains some of the most beautiful and natural golf courses in the north of England, ranging from championship length tests to short enjoyable courses with lots of character. All are worth a visit.

Alwoodley
Wigton Lane, Leeds (off A61). 0113 2681680. A fine lengthy heathland course with trees and heather. 18 holes, Par 72, SSS 72.

Ben Rhydding
High Wood, Ben Rhydding, (SE side of village). 01943 608759. Moorland course with splendid views of the Wharfe valley. 9 holes, Par 65. SSS 64.

Bradford
Hawksworth Lane, Guiseley, (SW of town centre off A6038). 01943 75570 Moorland course with eight par 4 holes of more than 360 yards. 18 holes, Par 71, SSS 70.

Bracken Ghyll.
In Addingham village on the old Skipton Road just off the A 65. 01943 830691. On reclaimed farm land, quite hilly. 9 holes, Par 74, SSS 72. Nine more holes are under construction.

Brandon
Holywell Lane, Shadwell, Leeds, (in village). 0113 2737471. Short parkland course, ideal for beginners. 18 holes mostly par 3s.

Cocksford
Cocksford Farm, Stutton near Tadcaster, 01937 834253. Flat parkland course with plenty of trees. 18 holes, Par 72 SSS 72.

Cookridge Hall
Cookridge Hall Lane, Otley Old Road, Leeds. 0113 2300641. Parkland course with water hazards. 18 holes, Par 71, SSS 71. Driving range.

Headingley
Back Church Lane, Adel, Leeds, (off A660). 0113 2675100. An undulating course with a wealth of natural features and offering fine views. 18 holes, Par 69, SSS 70.

A distinguished professor of Pathology who holed out in one at the fourth hole of his local course, thus opening his round with 4371444, asks whether he is the only man in history to have started a round of golf with his own telephone number.
Henry Longhurst

Ilkley

Middleton, Ilkley, (North side of river, off A65). 01943 600214. A parkland course which has the Wharfe as a hazard on the first five holes.18 holes, Par 69, SSS 70.

Leeds (Cobble Hall)

Elmete Lane, Roundhay, Leeds, (off A 58.) 0113 2658775. Parkland course with pleasant views.18 holes, Par 69, SSS 69

Moor Allerton

Coal Road, Wike, Leeds, (between A61 and A58). 0113 2661154. 27 holes on undulating parkland with ponds. Designed by Robert Trent Jones. Par 72, SSS 72. Driving range.

Moortown

Harrogate Road, Alwoodley, Leeds, (on A61). 0113 2686521. A flat heathland course that staged first Ryder Cup matches in Britain.18 holes, Par 71, SSS 72.

Otley

Off West Busk Lane, Otley, ($1^1/_2$ miles SW of town, off A 6038). 01943 461015. Well wooded with streams crossing the fairways. Magnificent views across Wharfedale.18 holes, Par 70, SSS 70.

Roundhay Park

Park Lane, Roundhay, Leeds, (off A 6120 Ring Road). 0113 2662695. Attractive municipal course in parkland, easy walking. 9 holes, Par 65, SSS 68.

Sand Moor

Alwoodley Lane, Alwoodley, Leeds, (off A61). 0113 2685180. A wooded, undulating course overlooking the Harewood estate and Eccup reservoir.18 holes, Par 71, SSS 71.

Scarcroft

Syke Lane, Scarcroft, (west of village). 0113 2892263. Parkland course, easy walking.18 holes, Par 71, SSS69.

Scarthingwell

Scarthingwell village, near Tadcaster, (Just off the A 162). New, flat parkland course. 18 holes, Par 72, SSS 72

Skipton

Off the North West By-pass,(1 mile N of town on A 65). 01756 793257. Grassland course with panoramic views.18 holes, Par 68, SSS 69.

Wyke Ridge

Wike Ridge Lane, Wike, Leeds, (off A61). 0113 2886000. Heath and moorland course. Can be windy. 18 holes, Par 72, SSS 72. Also 12 hole par 3 course and driving range.

Wetherby

Linton Lane, Wetherby, (1 mile W of town) 01937 62527. Parkland course with the river always in view. 18 holes, Par 71, SSS 70.

BREWING IN WHARFEDALE

O Yorkshire, Yorkshire: Thy Ale is so strong,
That it will kill us all if we stay long.

George Meriton *The Praise of Yorkshire Ale (1684*

Brewing in Yorkshire dates from Roman times and while early records are patchy there are some clear benchmarks in the county's brewing history and some of the more important ones are rooted in Wharfedale. The Bingley Arms at Bardsey near Leeds is a pub that makes a claim to be the country's oldest with a list of licensees dating back to 953 when Samson Ellis was recorded as its landlord and brewer. Brewing continued there up to 1942 when the plant was destroyed during an ARP exercise.

There are records of brewing in Tadcaster, the county's main brewing town, dating from 1341. The Samuel Smith brewery built in 1758 is the oldest one now operating in the county and is still in family ownership. Next door is John Smith's, built in 1884 and at one time related, but now part of the Scottish Courage empire. Across the town, is the former Tadcaster Tower Brewery dating from 1883 and now owned by Bass which completes the brewing trio of Tadcaster. Around the turn of the century there were two smaller breweries in Tadcaster: the Victoria Brewery in Chapel Street and the New Brewery. Both were acquired in1895 by Braimes Tadcaster Breweries Ltd. In 1903 this company amalgamated with Leeds City Breweries Ltd and the Tadcaster plants were closed down. In nearby Towton a small brewery owned by Daniel Stoker, was acquired by John Smith in1910.

In 1824 The Duke of Devonshire who owned most of Wetherby put 1,300 acres together with all the buildings and farms up for sale; it became known as the Great Sale of Wetherby. Gregory Rhodes, the tenant of the brewery in the Market Place bought the freehold of the brewery, a house, the maltings and five inns to start his own tied estate. Later he bought the Blue Anchor and when he died in 1829 his will showed the title of eighteen inns in an estate stretching from York to Otley. Ownership of the brewery then moved to Quentin Rhodes and the company was incorporated before 1837 as Quintin Rhodes and Co. Later, sometime between 1861 and 1892, it was owned by James Coates who registered it in 1896 as the Wharfedale Brewery Company to merge with the Eagle Brewery in Leeds. Brewing ceased early in the new century and the pubs were leased and eventually sold to the Leeds City Brewery.

Ilkley had a brief tryst with brewing. The Ilkley Brewery and Aerated Water Co. Ltd., started up in business in Brewery Road some time in the mid-nineteenth century. The brewery was acquired by Hammonds of Bradford in

1923 along with 37 tied houses. Bottled beers were sold under the Olicana trade mark. James Weatherill who was manager of the Ilkley Brewery in 1877 was also noted as brewing at the Ilkley Wells Brewery in Skipton Road in 1892 but little else is known about this firm.

Wharfedale's newest brewery opened in 1998 when, Doctor Paul Briscoe (01943 466515) started brewing in the cellar of his semi-detached house in Otley. He put his hobby of home brewing on to a commercial scale brewing 36 gallons each week which he racked off into nine gallon casks. He has since expanded and moved his plant into an outhouse of the Bowling Green pub. He is experimental in his beers and names them after events and places in the Dales: Chevin's Chaser, Rumbald's Reviver and Burnsall Classic are among them. He sells in the free trade in Otley and Leeds. Prior to this there has been no brewing in Otley since 1910 when the Cross Pipes pub closed down its brew house.

*H*OW BEERS ARE BREWED

*I*n its simplest form beer is made from water (which the brewer calls 'liquor'), malt, hops and yeast. Sometimes other materials may be added but the basic ingredients remain the same. Malt, usually malted barley, is ground to a rough flour - called grist - and then mashed with hot water in a mash tun. The natural sugars from the malt are extracted and disolve in the liquor to form what is now called the wort.

This is then boiled and hops are added in a vessel called a copper or kettle. After cooling the hopped wort is run into fermentation vessels and yeast is added. The action that follows converts the sugars into alcohol - in this case beer - and after settling this is drawn off into containers - casks, kegs, bottles and cans - for serving.

This is, of course, all very simplistic and there are many variations in both materials and the process. Grains other than barley such as wheat can be used and unrefined sugars are sometimes added at the mashing stage. Hops, which act as both a flavouring and a preservative, may be added at different stages, even after the brewing process has finished which is called 'dry-hopping.'

In some breweries fermentation takes place in what are called Yorkshire Squares which is claimed to give beers a smoothness and a fuller flavour. And there are different kinds of yeast. Those for making ales and stouts work on top of the cooled wort, whereas bottom fermenting strains are used for lagers and act at much lower temperatures and usually for longer periods. Lager is simply the German word for store.

Beer at its best remains a living thing and 'real ale' brewed almost exclusively in Britain is the classic example of this. At the other end of the scale beers are filtered and pasteurised and do not mature any further - keg and smooth beers are examples - and they lack character and style.

Real Ale:

A term coined by CAMRA meaning beer brewed from traditional materials, matured by a secondary fermentation in the cask and served without the use of extraneous carbon dioxide, usually by a handpump but occasionally by gravity. It is neither pasteurised or filtered. Also called 'traditional', 'cask' or 'cask conditioned' ale.

Yorkshire Squares

A system of fermentation originated by Timothy Bentley more than 200 years ago in the West Riding of Yorkshire. It is still used in three Yorkshire breweries as well as one in Lancashire and one in Nottinghamshire. The system utilises double decked vessels which were originally made of slate or stone and a chimney through which the fermenting wort is forced. Regular rousing is needed to get the best out of the yeast which in turn produces a full and smooth textured beer.

Pub Food In Wharfedale

Not too long ago the *Good Pub Guide* which tends to concentrate on the food qualities of pubs named Wharfedale as the best pub countryside in Britain. It said that '...at every turn there seems to yet another lovely pub'. In the latest edition 13 pubs from the dale are named, so the tradition continues. In the fifth edition of the popular *Good Pub Food* guide only three pubs get a mention and their licensees have been invited to submit a recipe that reflects the style and ingredients of Yorkshire and the Dales and, if possible, Wharfedale in particular. All the recipes will provide enough for eight or six or seven hungry tykes.

Ian Taylor at the Old Hall Inn at Threshfield has been in all five editions of *Good Pub Food*. He stresses that wherever possible local produce is used in his kitchen. One popular dish is an individual joint of Wharfedale lamb with port and redcurrant sauce. Another is Landlord's steak pie made with Taylor's ale. And he regrets that in the dish that follows the chickens were imported from Nidderdale. For **Braised Chicken with sun-dried tomatoes** you require:

2 lb diced chicken thigh meat	4 rashers of smoked streaky bacon in strips
25 grams tomato puree	Olive oil
4 sprigs of fresh rosemary	Half pint of dry white wine
8 sun dried tomatoes cut into strips	Salt and freshly ground pepper
6 cloves of garlic (roasted with olive oil	6 pints of good quality chicken stock
2 thinly sliced onions	Fresh basil

Heat a heavy based sauce pan and add a little olive oil. When hot add the chicken meat and seal all over. Remove from the pan and place in a casserole dish. Add the bacon to the hot pan, seal and cook for one minute. Add the sliced onions with the rosemary and cook until brown. Mix in the tomato puree, add the white wine, chicken stock and sun-dried tomatoes. Reduce this liquid by about half and then add to the chicken in the casserole dish. Braise in the oven for about $1^1/_2$ hours at 350° F, 180° C, Gas mark 4, season with salt and pepper and thicken if necessary. Finally chop the basil and add to the finished dish.

Jill Thorpe a former landlady at the Ferry Inn in Cawood was happy to share with us her recipe for **Beef and Stout Pie** one of the most popular dishes at the pub. But when asked for quantities she had a problem. 'I know how much of each ingredient to put in but I've no idea what they weigh,' she confessed. However with trial and error it was possible to come up with the following:

3lb chuck steak	Seasonings
$1^1/_2$ sticks of celery chopped	Shortcrust pastry
1 lb mushrooms	Egg and milk for glaze
1 pint stout	

Cut the steak into bite sized pieces and fry off until sealed. Place in a large saucepan and cover with water, bring to boil and then allow to simmer gently for 30 minutes. Add the celery for a further ten minutes and then the mushrooms and the stout and appropriate seasoning. Continue simmering for another 30 minutes. Spoon into a large deep pie dish or individual ones and seal with pastry. Jill uses what she calls demi-puff which is halfway between puff and shortcrust. But she sees nothing wrong with shortcrust and was persuaded to recommend it for this guide. Glaze with egg and milk and bake in a hot oven (425° F, 220° C, Gas mark 7) for 30 minutes or until the pastry is golden brown.

Hilary McFadyen at the Fox and Hounds at Starbotton was reluctant to pass on any of her recipes as she is presently working on her own cookery book which is awaited with confident expectation. Most of her food is home made including bread and ice cream. The menu includes a number of vegetarian choices and several interesting sweets including the fascinating sounding Yorkshire Hot Wine Pudding which she was persuaded to share with us and for which you need:

1 pint sweet sherry	Juice and rind of $1/2$ orange
4 eggs	1 ounce castor sugar
$1/2$ teaspoon cinnamon	2 packets of trifle sponges
1 ounce currants	1 ounce of butter (melted)

Break up the sponges into an oven proof dish and add all the other ingredients and mix well. Allow to soak for one hour and then bake in a medium oven (325° F, 160° C, Gas mark 3) for 30 minutes. Serve with custard, cream or ice cream. It will serve six or seven.

ᴾUB NAMES

Of the 150 pubs in Wharfedale the most popular names are the Fox and Hounds and the Red Lion with five each. They are followed by the Bay Horse, the Crown and the Devonshire with four each. Then with a count of three are the New Inn, the Old Star, the White Horse and the White Swan. The inclusion of the Red Lion and the Crown are not surprising for they are estimated to be the two most popular pub names in Britain. The New Inn, which is easily the most popular name in Yorkshire, and White Horse find their way into the national top twenty.

Some of the others have more interesting names, some are possibly unique. Take the Calcaria in Tadcaster which simply takes the Roman name of the town which could hardly be used elsewhere. Or the Spite at Newall near Otley which derives from a folk tale which is told on page 51. The Hermit at Burley Woodhead has a similar source which can be found on page 44. Situation often affects the name - the Ash Tree at Barkston Ash is close to where an Ash once grew that was said to be at the centre of the three ridings of Yorkshire. The Junction at Church Fenton is close by the railway junction whereas the Junction in Otley is at a road junction. The prefix Devonshire on four pubs comes from the family that owns much of the

Popular pub names – Crown Inn at Wetherby and The Bay Horse at Otley.

Popular pub names – Devonshire Arms in Cracoe (*Above*), Fox and Hounds at Starbotton (*Right*). and Red Lion in Bramham (*Below*).

land in the area that they are all found. And the Bingley Arms at Bardsey, England's oldest pub, was named after the family that owned the pub.

Some leave a question mark. Why for example are there three pubs called Old Star within a quite short distance of one another: East Keswick, Collingham and Clifford? Why is the pub at Thorp Arch called the Pax. There are several meanings for the word but it begs the question: which one and why? The present sign shows a dove, the bird of peace, and the Latin for peace is pax so it suggests that the owners are going for that defination. And

then there are pubs that take their names from famous people and linked with events such as the Admiral Hawke at Boston Spa or Duke of Wellington at East Keswick. It is likely though that the latter does not date from the Duke's victory at Waterloo in 1815 as one might think but his action in 1830 when Prime Minister in reducing the tax on beer!

Many pubs take their names from the animal kingdom: foxes, horses, birds, cattle, dogs and many others can be found. But few are individually recognised and the only one in Wharfedale is the Craven Heiffer at Addingham named after a 176 stone beast bred by a local vicar and that once graced the notes of a local bank.

Pubs In Other Guides

*M*any of the pubs in Wharfedale appear in other guides most of which are nationally based. Below is a list of those that do, showing which guides they are in.

Location	Name of Pub	GBG	GPG	GPF	RAI	TIW	PFF
Appletreewick	Craven Arms		X				
Appletreewick	New Inn	X					
Arncliffe	Falcon Inn					X	
Bardsey	Bingley Arms		X				
Buckden	Buck Inn		X			X	
Burnsall	Red Lion		X			X	
Cawood	Ferry Inn	X		X			
Cray	White Lion	X	X			X	
Grassington	Black Horse				X	X	
Grassington	Devonshire Arms					X	
Grassington	Foresters Arms					X	
Hebden	Clarendon					X	
Hubberholme	George		X				
Ilkley	Ilkley Moor Vaults	X					
Ilkley	Riverside Hotel	X					
Kettlewell	Blue Bell					X	
Kettlewell	Kings Head					X	
Kettlewell	Racehorses					X	
Kilnsey	Tennant Arms					X	
Linton	Windmill	X	X				
Linton in Craven	Fountaine		X			X	X
Litton	Queens		X			X	
Otley	Bay Horse	X					
Otley	Bowling Green	X					
Otley	Junction	X					
Pool in Wharfedale	White Hart		X				
Riffa	Hunters Inn	X					
Saxton	Greyhound	X					
Starbotton	Fox and Hounds		X	X	X		
Stutton	Hare and Hounds		X				
Threshfield	Old Hall Inn	X	X	X			
Ulleskelf	Ulleskelf Arms	X					
Wighill	White Swan						X

Index: GBG - Good Beer Guide; GPG - Good Pub Guide; GPF - Good Pub Food; RAI - Real Ale at the Inn; TIW - The Inn Way,; PFF - Pubs for Families.
All refer to the latest edition at the time of completion.

WHARFEDALE FROM THE AIR

*A*nyone who has flown out of the Leeds and Bradford airport will almost certainly have seen the River Wharfe appear over Otley Chevin and possibly watch Ilkley emerge just before your aeroplane vanishes into the clouds. You may be lucky and on a clear day the whole valley could be spread out before you. It depends, of course, on where you are bound for and how kind the weather is. However there are more certain ways of viewing Wharfedale from the air. Hiring a private plane from the airport is one but that could be

From the air looking north over Kettlewell to Moor End Fell

rather expensive. But helicopter rides and balloon flights are both available commercially on a regular basis.

Pennine Helicopters run pleasure flights from a number of locations through the summer including some half hour long ones from near Skipton which cover the valley from Grassington up to Cray and into Wensleydale. Flights are on most Sundays and bank holidays and occasional Saturdays. The company is based at Saddleworth in Greater Manchester on telephone: 01457 820152.

Airborne Adventures operate balloon flights daily from Settle and Skipton to several locations in the dales including Wharfedale. The company's base is at Rylstone near Skipton, telephone number 01756 730166. A similar service is run by Black Sheep Balloons from its base at Gargrave near Skipton, telephone: 01756 748106.

$\mathcal{A}$ Selection Of Wharfedale's Teashops

Addingham, in Main Street	*Good Food Shop*
Barden Tower	*Barden Tower Tea Rooms*
Bolton Abbey	*Bolton Abbey Tea Cottage*
Bolton Abbey	*Cavendish Pavilion Tea Rooms*
Bolton Abbey Railway Station	*Refreshment Rooms*
Bramhope, in Golden Acre Park	*Golden Acre Cafe*
Burnsall	*Wharfe View Tearooms*
Grassington	*Lucy Fold Tearooms*
Ilkley, The Grove	*Betty's*
Kettlewell	*The Cottage Tea Room*
Kilnsey	*Kilnsey Park and Trout Farm*
Lotherton Hall	*Stables*
Otley, Bridge Street	*Wharfe View Cafe*
Otley, Bondgate	*Cobblestones Tea Room*
Otley, New Inn Court	*Crowther's*
Otley, New Market	*Gloucester's*
Otley, Manor Square	*Manor Coffe House*
Storiths	*Buffers Coffee Shop*
Tadcaster, Bridge Street	*Teafare*
Tadcaster, High Street	*Claire's Pantry*
Wetherby, Horsefair Centre	*Perry's*
Wetherby, Market Place	*Rendevous Coffee Shop*
Wetherby, Shambles	*Bay Tree*

$\mathcal{T}$ourist Information Centres

Grassington	National Park Centre, Hebden Road	01756 752774
Ilkley	Station Road	01943 602319
Otley	Council Offices, 9 Boroughgate	01756 720311
Tadcaster	The Ark, 33 Kirkgate	01943 834113
Wetherby	Council Offices, 24 Westgate	01937 582706

 Public Transport

Railway services operated by Northern Spirit

Throughout the year trains run from Leeds to Ilkley on a half hourly service, Monday to Saturday, and an hourly service on Sunday. The Bradford (Forster Square) to Ilkley service is also half hourly from Monday to Saturday but two hourly on Sunday.

Both services have stops at Menston, Burley in Wharfedale and Ben Rhydding.

Services from Leeds to York sometimes stop at Church Fenton and very occasionally at Ulleskelf. It is best to check.

Bus services

Keighley and District Travel	01535 603284
Harrogate and District Travel	01423 566061
Horseless Carriage Services	01756 753123
Pennine Motors	01756 749215
Pride of the Dales	01756 753123
United Automobile	01325 468771
Yorkshire Coastliner	0113 244 8976
National Express	0990 808080

$\mathcal{U}$SEFUL WEB SITES

Bolton Abbey estate	www.yorkshirenet.co.uk/boltonabbey
Bradford Diocese CofE	www.bradford.anglican.org/index.htm
Campaign for Real Ale	www.camra.org.uk
Countryside Agency	www.countryside.gov.uk
Dalesman magazine	www.dalesman.co.uk
Embsay & Bolton Abbey Railway	www.yorkshirenet.co.uk/embsaybasteamrailway
English Heritage	www.english-heritage.org.uk
Grassington Festival	www.labcenter.co.uk/festival
Harewood House	www.harewood.org
Local bus and rail times	http://ukbus.u-net.co.uk
Lotherton Hall	www.leeds.gov.uk/tourinfo/attract/museums/lothert.html
National Trust	www.nationaltrust.org.uk
Ordnance Survey	www.ordsvy.gov.uk
Otley Folk Festival	www.otley-folkfest.demon.co.uk
Ramblers Association	www.ramblers.org.uk
Ripon and Leeds Diocese CofE	www.ourworld.compuserve.com/homepages/riponcc/
RSPB	www.rspb.org.uk
Yorkshire Tourist Board	www.ytb.org.uk
Youth Hostels Association	www.yha.org.uk
Yorkshire Agricultural Society	www.yas.co.uk

SHOWS AND FESTIVALS IN WHARFEDALE

Throughout the summer it is possible to find an agricultural show in a dales village every week. Wharfedale supplies its fair share and also hosts a number of arts events.

Mid May	Otley Show - the oldest in the dales (1796)
Mid May	Wharfedale Music Festival is held in Ilkley
Mid June	Bramham 3-day International Equestrian Event
Mid June	Otley Carnival
Mid June into July	Grassington Festival of the Arts (Two weeks)
Mid July	Arthington Show
First Sunday in August	Weeton Show
Mid August	Kettlewell Scarecrow Festival (Eight days)
Mid August	Burnsall Feast and Fell Race
Mid August	Harewood Show
Last Tuesday in August	Kilnsey Show
First Saturday in Sept	Bramhope Festival
Mid September	Otley Folk Festival (Three days)
Early October	Ilkley Literature Festival (Ten days)
First three Saturdays in December	Grassington Dickensian Festival
Mid December	Otley Victorian Fayre

Kettlewell Scarecrow Festival – The Vicar, Pilgrims Progress and Fill it up Sir?

THE COUNTRY CODE

Enjoy the countryside and respect its life and work
Keep dogs under control
Keep to public rights of way
Use stiles and gates to cross boundaries
Take litter home
Do not touch crops, machinery or livestock
Protect flora and fauna
Do not make excessive noise
Close gates behind you
Guard against risk of fire
Take care on country roads
Safeguard water supplies

Proof that country folk really are a welcoming crowd – signs at Appletreewick *(right)* and Eccup *(below)*.

HIKERS
MOUNTAIN BIKERS
CYCLISTS
HORSE RIDERS
WELCOME

WALKERS *Really Welcome*

$\mathcal{B}$IBLIOGRAPHY

Edmund Bogg, *Lower Wharfedale*
Nikolaus Pevsner, *The Buildings of England - Yorkshire West Riding*
Heliwell Sutcliffe, *The Striding Dales*
Arthur Mee, *Yorkshire, West Riding*
Mike Harding, *Walking the Dales*
Barrie Pepper, *A Haunt of Rare Souls*
Fred Baker, *Real Ale in the Craven Dales*
Richard Thompson, *North Yorkshire Ale*
Andy Ingle, *Bradford and District Beer Guide*
Denny Cornell, *CAMRA Real Ale Guide to Leeds*
Mark Reid, *The Inn Way*
CAMRA, *Good Beer Guide*, various editions
Alistair Aird, *Good Pub Guide*, various editions
Julia Smith, *Fairs, Feasts and Frolics*
A J Brown, *Striding through Yorkshire*
A J Brown, *Broad Acres*
W R (Bill) Mitchell, *J B Priestley's Yorkshire*
Eleanor Slingsby, *In Praise of Yorkshire*
Arnold Kellett, *The Yorkshire Dictionary of Dialect, Tradition and Folklore*
Arnold Kellett, *On Ilkla Mooar Baht at - The Story of the Song*
Val Leigh, *Discover some of the Churches of the Dales*
Lynn Pearson, *Building the West Riding*
Simon Jenkins, *England's Thousand Best Churches*
Alfred Wainwright, *A Dales Sketchbook*
Brian Morland, *Anglers Directory*

$\mathcal{T}$HANKS

Thanks are due to many of the licensees of pubs in Wharfedale for their kind assistance in helping to prepare this book. We hope they enjoy it and profit from it. A very big thank you goes to Christine Jopling for drawing the excellent maps. We are most grateful to the estate of J B Priestley for permission to quote three short extracts from his works and to Ian Taylor, Jill Thorpe and Hilary McFayden for providing recipes from their kitchens. And to our wives – Carolynne and Maggie – we give our love for their understanding and patience and invite them to yet another trip to our favourite dale. Cheers!

Barrie Pepper and Jack Thompson

Photographs
All the photographs are from Barrie Pepper's collection excepting those of the White Lion at Cray and the Bar t'at in Ilkley which were kindly loaned by the licensees.

Barrie Pepper   Jack Thompson

   BARRIE PEPPER is a journalist and author and Yorkshire's best known beer writer. He has been a member of the British Guild of Beer Writers since its formation in 1988 and for seven years was its chairman. He has written 13 books and been Highly Commended three times in the Beer Writer of the Year Awards.

   JACK THOMPSON has just retired after 28 years as an officer in the West Yorkshire Fire Service. Prior to that he spent 12 years in the Royal Marines. He is a regular contributor to his parish church magazine *St Aidan's News* and is presently working on a history of Leeds Fire Brigade. This is his first book.

Also by Barrie Pepper
   The Best Pubs in Yorkshire
   A Haunt of Rare Souls - a history of the Yorkshire pub
   The Bedside Book of Beer
   The Old Inns and Pubs of Leeds
   The International Book of Beer
   Irish Pubs
   Fifty Great Pub Crawls
   A Goodly Heritage - the history of St Aidan's church, Leeds

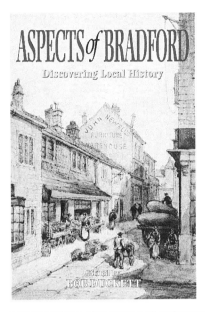

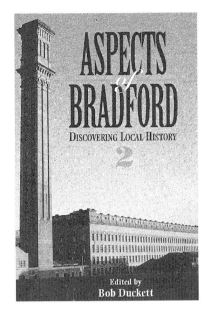

ASPECTS OF BRADFORD

Discovering Local History
Edited by Lynne Stevenson Tate

Law and Disorder in Medieval Bradford

The Tragedy of Jerry Delaney: Broomfield Hero

Thornton Village

Sorcerer's Apprentice: Pharmacy in Pre-war Shipley

On The Way To The Top: John Braine's Bradford

Burned to the Ground: Fires in Bradford's History

From Parcel Lad to Leylands: Trolleybus Tales

The Flying Boats of Bradford

Bradford's Italians

Keighley Pride

Saltaire: Vision to Vision

Favourite Haunts and Hidden Corners

ISBN: 1-87164-38-X – £9.95

ASPECTS OF BRADFORD 2

Discovering Local History
Edited by Lynne Stevenson Tate

Random Reverie: Memories of an Impressionable child

Eighteenth Century Life

School Days

Methodism in Bradford

Full Circle at Ilkley: Hydrotheraphy to Housecraft

Haworth Churchyard who were they?

Imprisoned for their Conscience: Keighley's Anti-Vaccination protest

The Glory of Lister Park: A Century of Enjoyment

H.L.B.I. and the Fountain Brewery

A Patients Lot at the Westgate Infirmary

James Burnley, The Saunterer's Satchel and the Bradford Literati

ISBN: 1-87167-82-7 – £9.95